faithgirlz

365 DEVOTIONS TO INSPIRE

GLIMMER & SHINE

BY NATALIE GRANT

To my Glimmer Girls: Bella, Gracie and Sadie
I love that you love God's word. Never
stop reading it, loving it, living it.

Other Books by Natalie Grant:

Contents

A Note
from Natalie

Hi there! Welcome to a year of devotion. I love God's Word. It helps me when I'm unsure, makes me feel safe when I'm afraid, comforts me when I'm sad, encourages me when I'm insecure, and instructs me on how to treat my family and friends. It's pretty much the most amazing guidebook for life. That's why I am so excited you're here! Because I believe it will be all those things and more for you. So take your time and learn more about who God is, and as you do, you'll learn more about who YOU are! The more you read, learn, and love God's word, it will help you glimmer and shine from the inside out!

It's going to be a great year!

Natalie Grant

SECTION 1

Be Forgiven

You wash me in mercy

I am clean

DAY 1

It's a good year to grow your relationship with God! What will you dare to be?

_____
_____
_____
_____
_____
_____

DAY 2

*Then the man and his wife heard the sound of the
LORD God as he was walking in the garden in the cool
of the day, and they hid from the LORD God among the
trees of the garden. But the LORD God called to the
man, "Where are you?"*

–GENESIS 3:8-9

For a while Adam and Eve enjoyed perfect harmony with their Creator in the Garden of Eden. But Satan changed it all with one bite of the forbidden fruit and sin entered human hearts. As the serpent slithered away, Adam and Eve hid. They felt ashamed.

Isn't that just like Satan? He hates being exposed, and he really hopes you never feel forgiven. So when we do something regretful, we often try to cover it up with lies, blame, and hiding. God shows his children a better way. He invites us into the light. He gives us a chance to come clean and be free. "Where are you?" he asks, not because he doesn't know exactly where we are or what has happened. Instead he's beginning a conversation. He's inviting us back into a relationship, where we can come out of hiding.

When we sin, the shadows seem safer. We don't want our sin in the light. But don't be fooled; don't hide. Instead, remember what Adam and Eve forgot: God is looking for you. He's inviting you to forgiveness and freedom. Go to him.

PRAYER Lord, thank you for loving me through my sin. Thank you for looking for me in the shadows and inviting me into the light. I confess to you. Restore me.

DAY 3

If the whole Israelite community sins unintentionally and does what is forbidden in any of the LORD's commands, even though the community is unaware of the matter, when they realize their guilt . . . the assembly must bring a young bull as their sin offering.

—LEVITICUS 4:13-14

Remember when you got in trouble when you were little? You'd do something wrong, get caught, and then turn your sweet face to your mom or dad. "I didn't know!" you might have said. Maybe your parents didn't buy the excuse, but they let you off the hook—at least that one time.

Back in the Old Testament, it didn't quite work like that. Even if people didn't know—for real—that they did something wrong, it was still sin. And sin separated them from God. Something had to be done. God told them exactly what to do once they understood they did wrong. He made a way back for them. What a gracious God!

In Jesus, God has made a way back for us. Maybe you believed your friends when they said an action wasn't wrong. Maybe you made a bad decision at school or you crossed other lines that friends or a TV show made seem okay. Then later you realized it was wrong. It's never too late. Talk to God and ask for his forgiveness. His grace is waiting.

PRAYER Lord, please show me if I have done something wrong without realizing it. I want to have a pure heart. Thank you that I can come to you with anything and find my way back to you.

DAY 4

He shall purify the house with the bird's blood, the fresh water, the live bird, the cedar wood, the hyssop and the scarlet yarn. Then he is to release the live bird in the open fields outside the town. In this way he will make atonement for the house, and it will be clean.

–LEVITICUS 14:52-53

Leviticus is a difficult book of the Bible to read. Don't worry if you find it hard. It's all about instructions for the priests of Israel who lived long before Jesus was born.

A holy God required offerings that proved the people were sorry for their sins. One of those sacrifices was to bring two birds to a priest. One was killed and its blood was mixed with water. This represented that death is the cost of sin. The other bird was allowed to live but was dipped in the bloody water before being set free. As it flew away, the live bird splattered the red liquid all around. This reminded the people that their sins had been paid for and their lives had been bought back by God.

Many years later, when Jesus died for our sins, there was no need to continue sacrificing animals. Jesus made the ultimate sacrifice, and his was perfect. But he didn't stay dead. That's what we celebrate at Easter. Jesus is alive again! The dead bird and the living bird in Leviticus remind us of Jesus. He paid for our sin, came back to life, and neither sin nor death is the end.

PRAYER Lord, I thank you that you covered my sins with your own blood. I'm also grateful that we don't have to perform all the difficult tasks like the Old Testament priests. I'm glad I can talk to you directly in Jesus' name!

13

DAY 5

The Lord said to Moses, "Say to the Israelites: 'Any man or woman who wrongs another in any way and so is unfaithful to the Lord is guilty and must confess the sin they have committed.'"

–NUMBERS 5:5-7

It's easy to get mad or annoyed and respond meanly to a friend, selfishly to a sibling, defiantly to a parent. When you get caught for disobeying, it definitely seems easier to deny it. The Israelites were like that too. In fact, everyone who has ever lived does wrong.

The best thing to do is exactly what God told the Israelites to do thousands of years ago: Admit it, tell the truth, and face it together. The truth is always better for you in the long run. Hiding your sin and making excuses will only cause more trouble. Confess, then make up. Go to the person you wronged or hurt. Say you're sorry. The Israelites had to apologize and return what they had taken or stolen plus one fifth more. That's not such a bad idea. What can you do to make up to someone today?

PRAYER God, I don't always think that telling the truth is the best because sometimes it's hard. But I know that lying or hiding my mistakes will cause more trouble. Please help me be quick about confessing my sin to you and to others I've hurt.

DAY 6

". . . In accordance with your great love, forgive the sin
of these people, just as you have pardoned them from
the time they left Egypt until now." The LORD replied,
"I have forgiven them, as you asked . . ."

–NUMBERS 14:19-20

Moses and God were close friends. But that doesn't mean it was always a smooth road. When God handpicked Moses to lead the Israelites out of Egypt, Moses wasn't wild about the idea. "I can't speak well," he said.

"I'll provide someone to help you," God replied.

"I can't do it," Moses said.

"I'll help you," God replied.

"Errgh," Moses said.

"Let's go," God said.

Moses and God talked all the time. When Moses recalled the Israelites' history of God's perfect love for the imperfect followers, he asked God to forgive them all, and God listened. The people faced consequences for sinful actions, but they wouldn't be eternally separated from their loving God.

Each one of us is invited to have a close, honest relationship with our heavenly Father, just like Moses had. It may not feel like a smooth road, but it is paved with love and mercy.

PRAYER
I can hardly believe that I can have an open, honest conversation with the living God. I'm not sure exactly what that looks like, but I will keep talking and listening to you, Lord, knowing that you will show me the way step-by-step.

DAY 7

John 3:17 makes it clear how God feels about the world. Find out what John says.

Unscramble the tiles to reveal the message.

S O	S E	O R L	E W	H I S	N D	T O	E W
I M	O N D	S A V	D B	O R L	F O R	O U G	H E
T H	I D	N O T	T H R	D D	G O	T H	N I
H H	E M N	E T	D T	L D	O C	W O R	U T
N T O

F O R	G O	to	his				

DAY 8

Jesus paid the price for our sins. List a few words that remind you of his loving sacrifice.

mom, dad, Luka,
Gaga, papa, Billy, Pia,

DAY 9

*These are the terms of the covenant the L*ORD*
commanded Moses to make with the Israelites in
Moab, in addition to the covenant he had made with
them at Horeb.*

–DEUTERONOMY 29:1

Covenant is a big word with a big meaning. It's a promise, a permanent agreement. Sometimes you'll hear a person say, "Cross my heart" when she promises to keep a secret. A covenant is a cross-your-heart kind of statement on steroids.

God made covenants often. He said, "I promise" several times to the people of Israel. As long as they followed him, God's promises were rock solid. He made a covenant to bless them with good crops, plenty of food, and a country of their own. He promised to care for them. He agreed to lead them. He even made a deal to bring a savior for the whole world out of their family. God made these covenants to prove over and over that he keeps his promises. Even when the people of Israel got tired of serving God, God still kept his end of the deal.

God is the ultimate promise maker and promise keeper. He sent his son, Jesus, to be the Savior. He offers forgiveness to anyone who asks. He takes care of all those who follow his ways. Are you ready to make a covenant with God? Once you do, you'll see how promise keeping changes your life.

PRAYER God, a covenant is a big deal. I accept your covenant of forgiveness. No one else can keep promises like you do. I want to be a person who keeps my promises. Help me to do that.

DAY 10

"But the thing David had done displeased the Lord."

−2 SAMUEL 11:27

David was a man after God's own heart (Acts 13:22). While he was a young shepherd, he wrote poetry inspired by the Almighty. David killed a fearsome giant while declaring his faith in God. David was handpicked by God to be king of Israel. And Jesus is one of David's descendants.

David loved God, and God loved David. But David wasn't perfect. The Bible reveals that David blew it . . . and then to cover his tracks, he blew it again . . . and again. Was God surprised? Nope. Was he displeased with David's choices? Yes. Did he want to give up on David? Not at all. God's love for us never changes, even when our behavior does.

David wasn't the only one who failed. Even the strongest pillars of faith in the Bible sinned. Jacob tricked his dad (more than once). Peter denied he knew Jesus out of fear (more than once). Abraham lied to protect himself (more than once). But God still loved them; he still chose to work through them in big ways.

God continues to use imperfect people with messy lives to do mighty things. He loves to heal, rescue, and reveal himself in our weaknesses. Stay close to him. He will use you too.

PRAYER Lord, I'm glad to see how you love imperfect people. I know I am imperfect too. Please use me to do your will.

DAY 11

*"This is what the L*ORD *says: 'Out of your own household I am going to bring calamity on you. Before your very eyes I will take your wives and give them to one who is close to you, and he will sleep with your wives in broad daylight. You did it in secret, but I will do this thing in broad daylight before all Israel.'" Then David said to Nathan, "I have sinned against the* LORD*." Nathan replied, "The* LORD *has taken away your sin. You are not going to die"*

–2 SAMUEL 12:11-13

Sometimes humans make up stories. Sometimes humans ignore problems. And sometimes they do both, which makes for a big mess. That's where we find King David.

The prophet Nathan rebuked David for a big mistake. David thought no one would know what he had done, so he pretended everything was okay. As soon as Nathan showed up, though, he called out David, leading David to repent. David confessed his sin and asked for forgiveness.

Nathan and God showed mercy to David after he showed sorrow over his wrongdoing. That's the way it works best. When you know you've done wrong, admit it. Even better, admit it before someone catches you. Honesty and repentance are always better than the denial game.

PRAYER
God, help me to live in honesty. But when I mess up, I don't want to get caught. Please teach me to always be truthful and to confess my wrongs quickly.

DAY 12

*" 'The parents eat sour grapes, and the children's teeth
are set on edge[.]' As surely as I live, declares the
Sovereign LORD, you will no longer quote this proverb
in Israel.*

–EZEKIEL 18:2-3

If you were watching your mom play volleyball, would *you* be
the one who gets sweaty? Of course not. Your mom might need
to towel off, but *you* wouldn't.

In Israel people were blaming their parents for strange things.
The proverb says that if the parents ate sour fruit, the kids were
the ones who puckered. Then they said the same thing about following God. They blamed their parents. "Well, my parents didn't
serve God, so now I'm suffering the consequences. No fair!"

True, living apart from God has consequences!

Thankfully, God says each person is responsible for her own
life. And each person is also responsible for her choice to follow
or not follow God. So even if your grandma didn't love God, it
doesn't affect *your* relationship with your heavenly father. Your
relationship with God depends only on you. You can love God and
live a blessed life because of your own choice and faith.

PRAYER

Lord, it's easy to blame others for my problems. And
sometimes I feel like I suffer the consequences of
other people's choices. Will you remind me that I'm
responsible for myself and my choices?

DAY 13

Who is a God like you, who pardons sin . . . You do not stay angry forever but delight to show mercy. You will again have compassion on us; you will tread our sins underfoot and hurl all our iniquities into the depths of the sea.

–MICAH 7:18-19

Chances are very good that you have had to forgive someone—maybe in the last day or even in the last hour! A friend may have acted selfishly. A family member may have made a careless mistake. A teacher might have hurt your feelings. Because people are not perfect, we are sure to get hurt. We may even hurt others sometimes too.

God demonstrates how to forgive. If anyone has a right to hold grudges, he does. He keeps his promises; we don't. He is faithful; we aren't. He loves perfectly; we don't. And yet his character is so full of love, grace, and mercy that he offers blessing and forgiveness. He doesn't give people what they deserve. He showers people with blessings. Over and over, he shows compassion.

If you've been betrayed, hurt, insulted, or teased, remember that Jesus was also. He knows exactly how it feels. He still says: forgive. And he's right there with you to help get you through it.

PRAYER It's hard to forgive. Sometimes I want to forgive, and sometimes I just don't. Help me have love and compassion even for those who hurt me.

DAY 14

Use the words of the verse that are not in bold to fill in the crossword puzzle. (Hint: Start with the longest word.)

"**I, even I, am he** who blots out your transgressions, for my own sake, and remembers your sins no more."

–ISAIAH 43:25

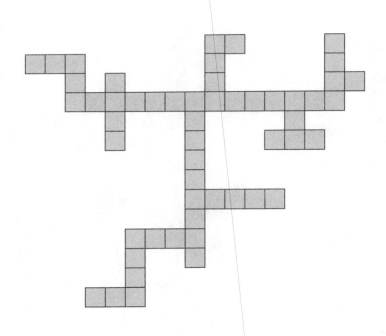

DAY 15

Being a Christian means being a "Little Christ." What are some ways you can be like Jesus?

_____
_____
_____
_____
_____
_____

DAY 16

Now Joshua was dressed in filthy clothes as he stood
before the angel. The angel said to those who were
standing before him, "Take off his filthy clothes." Then
he said to Joshua, "See, I have taken away your sin,
and I will put fine garments on you."

–ZECHARIAH 3:3-4

What makes you dirty? Playing sports outside? Camping with your family? A day at the beach? As soon as you finish a dirty activity, you probably rinse off in the shower. Maybe you scrub to get the dirt out from under your fingernails and then toss dirty clothes in the laundry.

After you get out of the shower, no one can tell what you did. You smell and look clean.

Sin gets us dirty too. Day to day, the sin leaves dirt under our spiritual fingernails. But for this kind of cleaning, a shower won't help one bit. Instead, this calls for the "God wash."

A dip in the sacrifice that Jesus Christ made on the cross. Then take the new set of "clothes" that are pure white. He will keep these garments clean with his own cleansing power. Spic and span, you are cleaned up from sin. Now that's a power wash! Thank God for his amazing plan to be our soul cleanser.

PRAYER Jesus, I praise you for the clean wash you give my life through your death. Thank you for saving me and forgiving all my sins.

25

DAY 17

Have mercy on me, O God, according to your unfailing love; according to your great compassion blot out my transgressions.

—PSALM 51:1

This verse is not the first time David calls out and asks for God's mercy. (It won't be the last time either.) David knew the Lord well and talked to him all the time.

When David prayed, he admitted he didn't know it all. He also considered God's character—his love, compassion, and mercy—the most valuable things ever to enjoy. David was in awe of how great the Father was, which made David realized he wasn't worthy of favor and approval. Forgiveness was made possible only by the character of God.

It's because *God* is worthy that we are brought into his kingdom on earth and in heaven. He loves us so much! We may feel far from him sometimes, but truly we are only one breath away. Talk to God. In your prayers you might do what David did: express your own heart—and think about God's heart for you.

PRAYER Lord, I'm so glad I can be open and honest with you about what I'm feeling, doing, and thinking. Thank you for your faithfulness and love that even though I mess up, you listen, love, and forgive.

DAY 18

*Cleanse me with hyssop, and I will be clean; wash me,
and I will be whiter than snow.*

−PSALM 51:7

Imagine never having to wash your face or your hair again!
Imagine being so clean that your hair has that shampoo-
commercial shininess and your skin has that sunshiny glow all
the time. Imagine that even after a workout your armpits smell as
fresh as your breath. And your toes are smelling as clean as your
shampooed hair. *That* is clean!

Clean on the *outside*. Everyone needs to give the *inside* attention as well. When you are a Christian, God is most interested on
the inside. And he starts work on your everyday actions and attitudes. You can try to clean yourself up by being good. And you
might feel pretty good for an hour or two—but then something
happens. You'll say something wrong or hurt someone's feelings
or pick up that bad habit. Before you know it, that "I messed up,
life is dumb, I'm not good enough" filth comes along.

God promises to take it all away. He cleans us up with a forever clean. Oh, you'll still have to face up to bad days or even bad
choices and ask God's forgiveness but you will know clean "I am
loved" joy from the inside out.

PRAYER Thank you, God, for cleaning me up. I know there's
not much I can do on my own, so thank you for loving
me and making me as white as snow. What a gift!

DAY 19

You, Lord, are forgiving and good, abounding in love to all who call to you.

−PSALM 86:5

If you remember anything, remember this: God is good—always. He forgives your sins—all of them. He loves you—beyond anything.

The Bible is God's love letter to his people and records their response to it. Over and over again, God proved his love, forgave wayward hearts, and reminded his people of his goodness. And they needed to be reminded a lot.

The Bible is full of people who forgot that the heart of God is always good. Adam and Eve suspected God was holding out on them. The Israelites whined when God freed them from slavery. They created idols to replace the living God. They rejected the Messiah sent for them. They constantly betrayed the one who loves them most. (We still do.)

Even with all that, God's loving kindness and faithfulness persisted throughout the Bible as it persists today. Don't forget, and don't be deceived into believing anything different. You may not understand his plan. You may not see everything clearly. So let this Psalm remind you: God is good. Always.

PRAYER What good news you share with your children, God! I praise you for your goodness and thank you for your trustworthy love. I'm so glad to be your beloved child.

DAY 20

If you, LORD, kept a record of sins, LORD, who could stand?

—PSALM 130:2-3

What if you were in charge of keeping a record of everything your parents did wrong? You'd have to follow them around and determine if what they did was a sin and write each thing down. You'd have to know their thoughts. Sometimes they might try talking you out of writing something down. Sometimes you'd be extra tough and sometimes you might miss one or two things. Your record of sins would be flawed. This is why we should not judge other people. Humans are not good at it.

But God, the one who has authority over sin and sinners, is the perfect judge. He knows each person's actions and sins, but he also knows each heart and thought. He sees everything clearly, all the time, inside and out. He's just and right, so his record is flawless.

When he judges in his perfectness, we are guilty as charged. We have no defense. We can't stand before him and claim to be innocent, because he knows the truth.

That could be the end of the story. But thankfully it's not.

Jesus, the only one who walked the earth without sin, paid sin's penalty for us. He was condemned to death in our place. He died for everyone. And if you were the only one who had ever sinned, he would have died just for you. Can you imagine such a friend?

PRAYER

I ask for forgiveness for my sins. Thank you, God, for wiping away the bad things I do and the things I leave undone. Thank you, Jesus, for this gift. I want to follow you and share the light of life.

DAY 21

Use the key to crack the code. When you're done, the letters in the boxes will spell out some godly traits.

The LORD our God is _____ and
_____ , even though we have
rebelled against him.

-DANIEL 9:9

A=1	F=6	K=11	P=16	U=21
B=2	G=7	L=12	Q=17	V=22
C=3	H=8	M=13	R=18	W=23
D=4	I=9	N=14	S=19	X=24
E=5	J=10	O=15	T=20	Y=25
				Z=26

G+F =

B+C =

J+H =

A+B =

G+B =

C+C =

L+I =

H+D =

D+B =

K+D =

I+I =

E+B =

F+C =

T+B =

H+A =

G+G =

C+D =

30

DAY 22

God loves you with a never-ending love. Write a note of thanks to him.

_____
_____
_____

DAY 23

"Come now, let us settle the matter," says the Lord. *"Though your sins are like scarlet, they shall be as white as snow; though they are red as crimson, they shall be like wool."*

—ISAIAH 1:18

If you've ever splattered spaghetti sauce, squirted ketchup, or dripped blood on a white shirt, you know it makes a stain. Your mom probably cringes at the idea of Kool-Aid or drippy Popsicles near white furniture or carpet. Once it stains, it's ruined.

While it's not hard to make something white turn red, God goes in the opposite direction. He takes what's stained and makes it clean. The Bible says once we believe in Jesus the stain of sin is turned "white as snow."

"Come now," he says. "Don't wait." Don't wait until you're older, wiser, better, nicer. Don't wait until you're more grown-up, more mature, more "churchy." "Come now and settle the matter," he says. Next time you see a photo of snow, picture yourself dancing and making snow angels in it, celebrating the good news of being without stain!

PRAYER Lord, I'm so glad that you make me and others clean, and you are excited to do it! Thank you for wanting to be friends with me.

DAY 24

Let the wicked forsake their ways and the unrighteous
their thoughts. Let them turn to the Lord, and he will
have mercy on them, and to our God, for he will freely
pardon.

—ISAIAH 55:7

Sometimes when we do something wrong, we want to do something good to make up for the bad. Have you ever felt like that? If you were mean to a friend, instead of saying you're sorry you'd rather just make it up by being extra nice. If you talked back to your mom, you act extra nice the next time you see her and maybe do some extra chores to make her happy. It's not unusual. It makes us feel better to earn our way back to favor.

If we think, "My good words earn God's love and forgiveness," we're getting it backward. Really, his love came first. Our devotion to him comes second. And we don't ever have to earn his affection.

PRAYER Lord, what good news that you love me just the way I am. Help me turn to you, live for you, live through you. With your forgiveness and grace, I am free to love you, myself, and those around me completely.

DAY 25

For if you forgive other people when they sin against you, your heavenly Father will also forgive you.

Say you had a favorite necklace that your dad gave to you. Because it's special, you take care of it and keep it in a safe place when you're not wearing it. How would you feel if your friend really wanted to wear it, you agreed just this once, and she broke it? How would you honestly feel? Maybe you'd feel she was careless or not sorry.

Today's verse reminds us that if you know Jesus, you have been forgiven. You've been released from God's anger. Feeling forgiven can stir up all sorts of positive feelings. It often brings peace and it certainly delights your Father in heaven. But once we're forgiven and accept God's pardon that means we have the responsibility to "pay it forward."

It's not always easy to forgive someone else. Sometimes it's really *hard*. But if you invite God into the process, talk with him, and seek his wisdom, *he* makes a way. Start by going to him.

PRAYER

Lord, sometimes I don't think other people deserve my forgiveness. But I know I didn't deserve yours. Help me do my best to follow your example and forgive. Help my heart embrace the gift you have freely given me.

DAY 26

A man with leprosy came and knelt before him and said, "Lord, if you are willing, you can make me clean." Jesus reached out his hand and touched the man. "I am willing," he said. "Be clean!" Immediately he was cleansed of his leprosy.

–MATTHEW 8:2-3

The disease of leprosy was very bad news in Jesus' day. Physically it was a long-lasting, uncomfortable condition. Emotionally it left patients completely alone and rejected because no one wanted to get close enough to catch it. Spiritually it made outsiders wonder, "What did that person with leprosy do to deserve God's punishment?"

So the man in the verse who approached Jesus was going out on a limb and taking a big chance. The man wasn't supposed to be in the crowd, but he wanted so badly to be healed. He came and expressed his faith. No one would've been shocked if the crowd pushed him away or if Jesus turned his back. What was shocking was Jesus' compassion. He reached out to the man, touched his loneliness, and healed his hurts.

Jesus never shrinks away from sickness or shame. He *always* offers healing and hope to *everyone* who comes to him with even the shyest of faith. Jesus touches the pain and says, "I'm here and I'm willing."

PRAYER
Lord, thank you for caring for people. Thank you for reaching out to me and being there for me.

DAY 27

Then Peter came to Jesus and asked, "Lord, how many times shall I forgive my brother when he sins against me? Up to seven times?" Jesus answered, "I tell you, not seven times, but seventy-seven times."

–MATTHEW 18:21

In the day of Moses' law, the prevailing wisdom was "eye for an eye and a tooth for a tooth." That is, a person's punishment should match the seriousness of the crime. The law served its purpose at the time because it made sure things didn't spiral out of control. For instance, if your sibling borrowed your shirt without asking, you could take *her* shirt, but you couldn't shred her favorite sweater. The law made sense to people and kept things fair.

Jesus turned the law upside down with his message of grace. Fairness went out the window and forgiveness took the place of revenge. When Peter asked Jesus how many times he should forgive his brother, he likely thought he had the handle on Jesus' radical idea. Not only did Jesus say to turn the other cheek, but he suggested forgiving someone *seven* times.

Even today Jesus encourages us to forgive so many times that we lose count (the same amount as he forgives us, by the way). He loves it when we stop keeping score and rally in grace.

PRAYER Lord, I like things to be fair, but you want me to forgive. Help me to embrace the difference. I want to please you, but I need your help.

DAY 28

Search up, down, and sideways to find the bolded words in the verse below.

And **forgive** us **our debts**, as we **also have forgiven** our debtors.

```
S D H R H F Q V I W U Z K M M
I E H D S N O L R O S V A F B
C B K R S Y O R Z J Z P D R G
Q T U G H F O R G I V E N X R
I O Q K L F L S W I B P W Y V
W R U K D C Z M F T V E V V N
F S B D V F X O S U E I Z W
P Q G S K J P I B I K Y A X K
F W Q Q H K C I I L V H E Q E
G D L R W Y M Q W O B Q W U Y
S N W N W Y P I S X L W B F N
R A U P X G C U I G Q E C Z X
A Y N B N X M X A R V J V E M
T T Y W U F E M C A S F D A S
N N J Q A G L T O S L A B L H
```

ALSO
AND
DEBTORS
DEBTS
FORGIVE
FORGIVEN
HAVE
OUR

DAY 29

Jesus' love is like an anchor. What other metaphors or words can you think of to describe Jesus' love and friendship?

_____

_____

_____

_____

_____

DAY 30

"This is the blood of the covenant, which is poured out for many for the forgiveness of sins."

−MATTHEW 26:28

Remember covenant means contract or promise? It's an agreement between two parties that says, "I will do this. In return you will do that."

In his grace, God came up with a covenant with people. It's spelled out in John 3:16. "For God so loved the world" that he initiated a contract. "He gave his only son" to pay for the sins of the world. In return, "whoever believes in him will have everlasting life." God gave his son as a sacrifice. Jesus paid for sin on the cross. In return his people have faith in him, follow him, and are granted everlasting life.

The night before Jesus died, he poured red wine in a cup. It was a symbol of the blood that was about to be poured out on the cross. If you have experienced communion at church, then you've been reminded of God's great covenant, his great sacrifice, his great love.

God has never broken his promise. Even when we are faithless, God is faithful.

PRAYER

Thank you, God, for your promise of eternal life. Thank you that you made it possible by sending your son. I trust you and want to follow you.

DAY 31

*The angel said to the women, "Do not be afraid, for I
know that you are looking for Jesus, who was crucified.
He is not here; he has risen, just as he said. Come and
see the place where he lay."*

—MATTHEW 28:5-6

The followers of Jesus had just faced the worst day of their
lives. Soldiers and angry crowds had killed Jesus. The
disciples were scared for their own lives. They had no idea how
this would turn out.

Just three days later, something that had never happened
before happened!

Jesus rose from the dead. His death was part of God's plan.
The disciples thought his death was the end. They didn't have the
entire New Testament to read, so they didn't know how the story
went. God had planned a grand miracle. Resurrection! Taking
down death with life. The death and resurrection of Jesus Christ
was the most awesome event ever. Even angels were involved in
the plan.

Amazing that the God who knows all allows us to be part of
this celebration. Trusting his great plan, really trusting him every
day, is an adventure. And God will never leave us alone on that
journey.

PRAYER Thank you, God, for Jesus' life and death and life
again. Please help me as I follow the ways of Jesus.
Remind me each day of the big plan you have for my
life, even when I can't see everything right away.

DAY 32

Immediately the rooster crowed the second time. Then Peter remembered the word Jesus had spoken to him: "Before the rooster crows twice you will disown me three times." And he broke down and wept.

−MARK 14:72

Peter was a special man. He followed Jesus with a lot of energy and was the first guy to step up. Sometimes, though, Peter's boldness got ahead of his brain. He was, of course, the disciple who said, "I will never disown you, Jesus," just hours before he said he didn't know Jesus three times in a row. Oops!

It's easy to wonder how Peter could do such a thing. What was he thinking? Unfortunately, we're no different. We promise to be friends with everyone and then just don't have enough energy to welcome the new student. We decide we're not going to put others down and then say bad things about someone who is annoying us. Everyone makes mistakes—even followers of Christ. The crazy thing is Jesus knows us better than we know ourselves. Even after Peter denied him, Jesus still loved Peter.

Peter went on to make a big strides for Jesus, even with all the missteps. Peter's hope in the Savior's love and acceptance kept him moving forward. If you've messed up, remember God still loves you and has big plans for your life.

PRAYER Jesus, I'm so glad you give second chances. Please forgive me when my words or actions deny you. Give me the courage of Peter to boldly tell others about your goodness.

DAY 33

After taking the cup, he gave thanks and said, "Take this and divide it among you. For I tell you I will not drink again from the fruit of the vine until the kingdom of God comes." And he took bread, gave thanks and broke it, and gave it to them, saying, "This is my body given for you; do this in remembrance of me."

—LUKE 22:17-19

Jesus and his friends were having dinner together. But it wasn't an ordinary meal. It was Passover. For Jews, Passover was a big deal. Like Thanksgiving dinner, they were sitting around the family table. In addition to eating, they were thanking God for the amazing things he had done.

This was Jesus' last Passover before dying and returning to heaven. He wanted to help his disciples understand what his death on the cross would mean. So he passed around a cup of wine (symbol of a covenant being made). Then he broke off pieces of bread and passed them around. He used the food to tell them that he was going to bleed and his body would be broken.

Ever since that Passover meal, Christians remember this Jewish feast. Today many Christians call it communion or the Lord's Supper. It's not a Sunday snack but a serious time to remember what Jesus did for us and give thanks to God for sending Jesus to earth so we can celebrate God's victory.

PRAYER Lord, thank you for the special meal we call communion. Whenever I see the cup and bread, I remember Jesus' blood and body that you sacrificed for me.

DAY 34

Jesus said, "Father, forgive them, for they do not know what they are doing." And they divided up his clothes by casting lots.

–LUKE 23:34

We all have moments that are not so pretty. Sometimes we get caught up in what's happening in life and we love things more than we love God. We love others a little but not as much as we love ourselves. It's hard to always be joyful and kind, especially when there are a thousand things to get done or people to talk to. Even with all of our excuses or reasons, God says, "I love you. I've loved you before you were even born. You can't do anything to make me love you less."

God's love letter to us: Jesus.

Jesus' love message to God: forgive them.

And God continues to forgive, continues to do great things. He knows you at your worst and still loves you at his best—with faithful forgiveness.

PRAYER

Thank you, Jesus, for dying on the cross to show your undying love for me. Sometimes it's hard to believe that you are on my side when I mess up. Thank you for reassuring me through your words in the Bible. I'm so glad you love me. I love you too.

DAY 35

Write the answer to each clue in the boxes below. When you're done, the letters in the shaded boxes will reveal what God does faithfully for those who follow him. (You might know some answers but for others, check out the verse below.)

For as high as the heavens are above the earth, so great is his love for those who fear him; as far as the east is from the west, so far has he removed our transgressions from us.

–PSALM 103:11-12

1. Our _____ , in heaven, hallowed be your name

2. He _____ our transgressions

3. Reverence, respect, be afraid of _____

4. As _____ as the heavens are above the earth

5. God is the great "_____ Am"

6. Great is his _____

7. The opposite of west _____

8. Another word for transgressions _____

DAY 36

What are some of the amazing things God is doing in your life?

_____
_____
_____
_____
_____
_____

DAY 37

"We are punished justly, for we are getting what our deeds deserve. But this man has done nothing wrong." Then he said, "Jesus, remember me when you come into your kingdom." Jesus answered him, "I tell you the truth, today you will be with me in paradise."

—LUKE 23:41-43

Two criminals hung on crosses next to Jesus. One mocked the Savior like many people in the crowd. "Aren't you the Messiah? Save yourself and us!"

The other criminal saw Jesus with clear eyes and a humble heart filled with questions and wondering.

This criminal *earned* his place on the cross. The criminal was paying for his sins by dying. We don't know what he did specifically, but even he knew that he deserved his punishment. He also knew that Jesus had done nothing to deserve death on a cross.

Jesus was innocent, convicted during an unjust trial. But that was God's plan. Jesus came to earth specifically for the cross. He was the unblemished lamb to be sacrificed. Even the criminal next to him knew it. "Jesus, remember me," he said.

This criminal had not earned a pardon for his actions. He simply came to Jesus. Immediately, Jesus gave him the Good News. Together they would be in paradise.

PRAYER Lord, even though you are forgiving, sometimes I still think I have to earn my way to heaven. Remind me that you've already paid the price for me. Now, instead of making sure I do more good things than bad, I can just follow you.

DAY 38

Repent, then, and turn to God, so that your sins may be wiped out, that times of refreshing may come from the Lord, and that he may send the Messiah, who has been appointed for you—even Jesus.

—ACTS 3:19-20

L et's talk about some of the words in this verse. They are full of promise and goodness, and you don't want to miss these game changers.

The first word: Repent means return, as in turn around, make a U-turn from sin. It's like a personal invitation from the Lord who says, "You don't need to go there. That way is a dead end. Instead come with me."

God promises to give rest to the weary, make the unwashed clean, make the broken whole. Have you ever been sick with a horrible cold for days . . . and then woke up feeling better? Or been super worried about something . . . and then received good news? The relief is amazing.

Here's a second word: Messiah. It means the one who saves, your champion, your defender. Jesus, the Messiah, is the only one who can redeem you. And it all starts with a U-turn.

PRAYER

Lord, I take your invitation to come away with you. I want to focus on you, your faithfulness, and your saving grace. Show me when I wander off, because I want to return to you.

DAY 39

And that is what some of you were. But you were washed, you were sanctified, you were justified in the name of the Lord Jesus Christ and by the Spirit of our God.

–1 CORINTHIANS 6:11

What if you dipped your toe in a mud pit? When you found out how soft it was, you stepped right in and—what's the harm really—sat in it . . . then laid in it . . . and rolled around . . . and slicked your hair back . . . and covered your face with all that mud. Maybe you were having fun at first, but as you stepped away, you realized the mud was stuck on and caked up! Rubbing it off only meant rubbing it in! It started as some innocent fun, but you quickly became a mess! You would need some serious help to get clean.

When we dip our toe into sin, it usually doesn't seem like a big deal. But it has a way of getting up around our eyes and ears and smearing up our hearts. When we realize that we're a mess and ask for help, thankfully Jesus doesn't stand there shaking his head at our dirty selves. Instead he hoses us off. He gives us clean white towels, and puts his arm around us.

PRAYER Lord, sometimes I don't want to show you how much mud I've gotten into. I'm relieved that you can wash me clean. Thank you for dying on the cross to make me new.

DAY 40

In him we have redemption through his blood, the forgiveness of sins, in accordance with the riches of God's grace.

–EPHESIANS 1:7

God is full of power and might. God is full of justice. He's full of righteousness. His character has many different and unique angles. He is full of power *and* full of love. He is full of righteousness *and* full of mercy. He is full of justice *and* full of grace. And we are eternally blessed because of it.

We can learn something from the riches of God's character. These riches have nothing to do with gold and trophies, fancy cars or ultimate houses. These riches have everything to do with things you give away to others—love, mercy, and grace.

PRAYER Thank you, God, for being so good and loving. Because of you, I can have can life in the riches of God's grace. Help me practice receiving your gifts and then passing them on.

DAY 41

Be kind and compassionate to one another, forgiving
each other, just as in Christ God forgave you.

–EPHESIANS 4:32

What if you went into the kitchen and saw your sibling sneaking a freshly baked cookie off the counter, one that your mom just said not to have! You'd have reason to be mad, right? After all, you were being obedient even though you really wanted a cookie too! But you would never sneak anything! You were so clearly right, and your sister was so clearly wrong. She deserves to feel badly.

Except . . .

Except Jesus took all brokenness to the Cross. He died for "little" sins and "big" ones, for open ones and secret ones, for planned-out ones and thoughtless ones, for ones done by your sister, for ones done by you. Your sin may not be the same as anyone else's, but we're all connected in our brokenness.

When you see how you and your sister are alike (broken and forgiven), it's easier to feel understanding and kindness. You both will feel the darkness of sin and the lightness of forgiveness.

Next time you witness something that is unjust or wrong, take your forgiven self over and offer compassion and kindness. Jesus will take care of the rest.

PRAYER

Lord, I sometimes think I'm better than people who sin differently than I do. But I realize you died for me as much as anyone. Because you give me loving kindness every day, I can practice doing the same. I'll need your help.

DAY 42

Use the words of the verse to fill in the crossword puzzle.
(Hint: Start with the longest word.)

Then he adds: "Their sins and lawless acts I will remember no more."

–HEBREWS 10:17

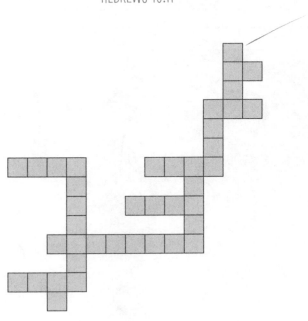

DAY 43

When I remember God is on my side, I feel like I can . . .

_____
_____
_____
_____
_____
_____

DAY 44

*For he has rescued us from the dominion of darkness
and brought us into the kingdom of the Son he loves,
in whom we have redemption, the forgiveness of sins.*

–COLOSSIANS 1:13-14

Picture yourself in your room at night. The door is closed, and even though your eyes are open, it feels like you're blindfolded. You put out your hands so you won't stub your toe as you slowly work your way across the room to the door. Because your eyes are blinded, your ears work overtime, hearing every little bump and creak. The longer it takes to find the door, the more afraid you get.

Now picture yourself in your room at night. This time your room is dark, but the lamp in the hallway is shining under the door. Even that small shaft of light cuts through the darkness. Keeping your eyes on the light, you make your way out quickly and without fear. Darkness cannot stand up to even the smallest source of light.

Jesus is called the Light of the World because he pierces the darkness of sin. He shines his light into fear and death and shows us the way out—his Son. We are no longer captives of the dark. We no longer have to stumble around finding our own way out. We've been rescued. We just have to follow the Light.

PRAYER Lord, thank you for your light that shines in the darkness. I confess my sins to you, because I know that your faithful forgiveness brings light to every corner of my life.

DAY 45

Bear with each other and forgive one another if any of you has a grievance against someone. Forgive as the Lord forgave you.

–COLOSSIANS 3:13

If your sibling makes fun of you in front of his friends, God agrees that's mean. If your best friend says something unkind about you behind your back, God is as unhappy as you. He doesn't shrug off your feelings. He knows it hurts. "But now," he says, "let's go a different way together."

Instead of holding on to your frustration, he wants you to embrace forgiveness and mercy. This is super hard to do by yourself—but you have the Holy Spirit!

So here's how you start: Let out all your grief and anger to God. Tell him what happened and how it made you feel. And then take a deep breath. Thank him for listening. Tell him that you really want to do what *he* wants you to do, that you will trust him with all the results, and that you might just need him to soften your heart as you wait. And then listen awhile.

If you stop scratching at your wounds, and let God bind you up, he will lead you to forgiveness because it leads to freedom. And wouldn't that feel a lot better than hurt and frustration

PRAYER
I get frustrated and hurt when someone is unfair to me. Thank you that I can come to you and you will take care of everything in your perfect way.

DAY 46

But when the goodness and loving kindness of God our Savior appeared, he saved us, not because of works done by us in righteousness, but according to his own mercy, by the washing of regeneration and renewal of the Holy Spirit, whom he poured out on us richly through Jesus Christ our Savior.

—TITUS 3:4-6

If you ever doubt that the heart of God is good, then go back through this verse. Get a pen, find every description of him, and circle it, underline it, or make squiggly lines coming out of each word like rays of sunshine. Go ahead. Take a minute.

This verse describes God as good, loving, kind, righteous, merciful. And because of Him, we are rescued, washed, renewed, and given the Holy Spirit. We didn't have to save ourselves, and we aren't alone. This is good news from a good God.

If to get on God's good side, we had to be good enough, strong enough, patient enough for long enough, it would be very bad news because we will never be enough. So our God made a way to him that takes the pressure off us. He has taken care of it all—he gave us Jesus. Because of Jesus, we are his unblemished children. Because of the Holy Spirit, God remains with us.

PRAYER

Lord, I love you and am grateful for your generous heart. Thank you for showing your faithfulness through Jesus and the Holy Spirit.

DAY 47

And where these have been forgiven, sacrifice for sin is no longer necessary.

–HEBREWS 10:18

At the beginning of the Old Testament, the Garden of Eden was stained by evil. Adam and Eve's disobedience put a wall between us and God. If God and people were to be reunited, a payment had to be made. It was no small price: sin equals death so a death had to happen. In the Old Testament, before Jesus came to earth, people and priests sacrificed spotless lambs. As people kept sinning, they had to keep making sacrifices.

Then, at the beginning of the New Testament, the ultimate sacrifice came to Earth. Jesus was the spotless Lamb of God. When his blood spilled on the cross, the price for sin was paid in full, completely, forever. The wall between us and God was shattered on the cross.

Genesis 22:8 says: "God himself will provide the lamb . . ." And we are so grateful he did.

PRAYER What a loving God you are to pay the debt for my sin. I am grateful that you made a way to get close to you. Help me walk in your ways.

DAY 48

If we confess our sins, he is faithful and just and will forgive us our sins and purify us from all unrighteousness.

−1 JOHN 1:9

The Lord is the King of all kings, but he doesn't just sit on a throne looking down at his subjects. He is a ruler, but he doesn't just stand at a distance making laws. He is a leader, but he doesn't just think about the big picture. Instead he has closed the space between us. He has invited us into a relationship, a two-way street, a give-and-take. He asks us questions, wants to know what we think, wants to be involved.

Part of our relationship is being honest and open, so we confess our sins. It's not like we're saying, "Hey, Lord, news flash: I cheated during the game yesterday." Really, he already knows, but he's reminding us, "Talk to me. Let me be your friend and watch me work this out for you."

It's one way the sinner and the King connect in relationship. He invites us to get close. We get closer by confessing. He gets closer by forgiving (every single time).

You've been invited by the King himself to join in and play a part. Will you participate in the relationship or let it pass you by?

PRAYER

Lord, thank you for welcoming me into a relationship with you. I'm grateful that I don't have to hide from you. I'd rather be close. I'm so glad you want to be close too.

SECTION 2

Be Changed

Even if you've lost your way

Turn and you will hear love say

You were made for more

DAY 50

Do you like change or do you fear it? What kind of changes do you seek?

_____

_____

_____

_____

_____

_____

_____

_____

DAY 51

"Please accept the present that was brought to you, for God has been gracious to me and I have all I need." And because Jacob insisted, Esau accepted it.

—GENESIS 33:11

From the beginning, Jacob had serious issues with his older twin, Esau. Their fighting drove their mom crazy. Jacob eventually stole Esau's future inheritance then took off when Esau made plans to kill him.

Years later Jacob got news that Esau—manly, hairy, hunter Esau—was headed his way. This time, however, Jacob didn't run. After praying for God's help, Jacob rounded up hundreds of animals to send to Esau as a peace offering. When the warring brothers finally reunited, Jacob threw himself to the ground.

"Let me find favor in your eyes," Jacob humbly asked his brother, and Esau accepted.

Your siblings may not raid your college fund, but they might break your stuff, embarrass you in public, or wrongfully blame you for things you didn't do. In return, you may want revenge. Yet acting like Jacob or Esau doesn't pay off. Instead, be the new and improved version of Jacob and Esau: two guys willing to confess their flaws, forgive, and start over. Maybe that doesn't involve giving sheep and goats to your family members. But how about offering the remote control (or front seat) along with a genuine "I'm sorry"?

PRAYER God, you forgive me for my mistakes. Please help me admit when I've blown it, make things right with those I've wronged, and forgive those who have hurt me.

DAY 52

*The LORD said to Moses, "I have heard the grumbling
of the Israelites. Tell them, 'At twilight you will eat
meat, and in the morning you will be filled with bread.
Then you will know that I am the LORD your God.'"*

–EXODUS 16:11–12

When the Israelites were freed from Egypt, they saw some jaw-dropping miracles from God. Pillars of fire, splitting seas, crazy plagues—it was like a modern day 3-D adventure film.

But the Israelites were not happy with that supernatural food that showed up when their stomachs growled. Instead of asking God for help, the Israelites complained. "Think of how good we had it in Egypt as slaves!" they moaned. "We had all the food we wanted."

Of course, God already had a plan to feed his children. That evening, a boatload of quail appeared for dinner while manna (a type of sweetened wafer) appeared on the ground for breakfast. All the Israelites had to do was pick it up and eat.

You might think the Israelites' whining was silly, but how often do we complain? Even though the Lord has provided many things for our lives, how often do you get grumpy about what you have and think it's not enough? Try praying instead of whining and see what happens. After all, miracles are a piece of cake—or manna—from our all-powerful, all-loving God.

PRAYER Lord, please forgive me for complaining. I want to trust you completely and have patience as I wait for my "manna."

DAY 53

When a man makes a vow to the LORD or takes an oath to obligate himself by a pledge, he must not break his word but must do everything he said.

—NUMBERS 30:2

Scene: Your dad promised you a trip to the movies if you earned all As. You earned the As and get ready to go. But when you excitedly remind him, he looks at you blankly. "I'm sorry," Dad says. "I'd rather go fishing than keep my promise to you." How would you feel? Would you believe him the next time he promised to do something for you?

Now answer this: Have you ever done the same thing to God? You certainly haven't taken him to the movies, but maybe you vowed to read your Bible every day if he helped you make the soccer team. Then you forgot. Or you promised to talk to a friend about the Bible but chickened out.

Breaking promises goes against God's nature. God never says one thing and does another. He never misleads or lies to us. That's why God told the Israelites to keep their promises. It's straightforward: Don't make a promise if you can't keep it. When you make a vow, keep it.

PRAYER

Thank you, God, for keeping all your promises. I want to do that too. Instead of speaking too quickly, help me weigh my words, and follow through with my actions.

DAY 54

If you hear it said about one of the towns the L<small>ORD</small> your God is giving you to live in that troublemakers have arisen among you and have led the people of their town astray, saying, "Let us go and worship other gods" (gods you have not known), then you must inquire, probe and investigate it thoroughly.

–DEUTERONOMY 13:12-14

Your friend tells you about a Brazilian girl with the longest hair in the world. She tells you that the girl's hair is eighteen feet long. Would you believe her? Outrageous stories or facts are hard to believe. So you'd probably ask your mom or dad. Or you'd go online to check out the *Guinness Book of World Records*.

Instead of believing everything you hear, check out the facts. Even God told the Israelites to investigate. Any time they heard a story, a rumor, a big tale, they were to find out the truth. God didn't want the Israelites to be fooled, especially when someone made up something about him.

The tricky part is that often rumors or big claims include *pieces* of the truth. For example, your friend telling you about the longest hair had one fact correct and one wrong. So put on your investigator hat. Dig up the truth from the experts. When it comes to God, use the Bible as your ultimate source.

PRAYER God, I don't want to be gullible and believe everything I hear. When it matters, will you show me where to go for the truth?

DAY 55

Satan rose up against Israel and incited David to take a census of Israel. So David said to Joab and the commanders of the troops, "Go and count the Israelites from Beersheba to Dan. Then report back to me so that I may know how many there are."

–1 CHRONICLES 21:1-2

Most countries count how many people they have every few years. In King David's time, however, there weren't any formal head counts. God wanted the Israelites and their leaders to trust in him, not in how many fighting men or chariots they had.

But David got prideful. His military was strong, his people happy, and his kingdom fairly secure. So when Satan planted a bug in his royal ear, David gave in to temptation and ordered a census. He wanted to sit back and say, "I've got a huge palace and this many men ready to protect me. Yep, we're pretty awesome."

What about you? You might be someone after God's own heart, just like David. Yet the king proved that he wasn't Satan-proof; he still had some lessons to learn and needed be on guard for temptation.

Be careful not to get caught up in your own brains, looks, body, or talents. Those things are temporary, but your relationship with God is forever.

PRAYER David wasn't perfect, and I'm not either. But God, I still want to be like him, asking for forgiveness when my love for myself tops my love for you. Teach me to be humble.

DAY 56

Write the words of the verse in the crossword puzzle. (Hint: Start with the longest word.)

"Do not conform to the pattern of this world, but be transformed by the renewing of your mind"

–ROMANS 12:2

DAY 57

Today I am thankful for:

_____

_____

_____

_____

_____

DECLARE THE PRAISES OF HIM WHO CALLED YOU OUT OF DARKNESS INTO HIS WONDERFUL LIGHT.
1 PETER 2:9

DAY 58

He did evil in the eyes of the LORD his God and did not humble himself before Jeremiah the prophet, who spoke the word of the LORD. He also rebelled against King Nebuchadnezzar, who had made him take an oath in God's name. He became stiff-necked and hardened his heart and would not turn to the LORD, the God of Israel.

–2 CHRONICLES 36:12-13

Zedekiah was young when he was crowned king of Israel. But age was not Zedekiah's problem. What messed up this young king's life was his inability to learn from, and in some cases, obey those who were over him. He resisted the king before him, the prophet, and God himself.

As you continue to read the Scriptures, you will discover that respecting authority is a characteristic of a godly person. The reason is clear. God places people in power over us. He does that to help us learn and grow. We need help to make right decisions. We also need others to coach us as we learn from mistakes.

Learning to respect an authority figure is a lifelong process. It doesn't come naturally or easily. Typically the first step in this process is obeying your parents, then grandparents, aunts, uncles, babysitters, teachers, and the list goes on. The most important thing to remember is when you respect elders, you are also obeying the Lord.

PRAYER Lord, sometimes I resist being told what to do. I want to be my own person. All the same, I understand you place authority figures in my life for a purpose. Give me the desire to cooperate.

DAY 59

But to the wicked person, God says . . . You use your
mouth for evil and harness your tongue to deceit. You
sit and testify against your brother and slander your
own mother's son.

−PSALM 50:16, 19−20

Have you ever gotten so angry you yelled, "I hate you"? Maybe you didn't actually say it but you thought it. Words are powerful. Even if you try to take back negative words once you've calmed down, what you say can hurt others. There really are no "take backs." Words are remembered for a long time.

Everyone makes mistakes with their words. It's often good to practice biting your tongue—literally—so your words won't harm others. Runaway words, things you say in the heat of an argument or stressful situation—can create a lot of trouble. It's okay to speak the truth, but be mindful and choose your words carefully. If hurtful words are bubbling to your lips, run to a place where you can be alone. Then spill them out to God. He wants to hear your honest heart. Once you've let it out to your heavenly Father, ask him to give you wisdom about how to handle the situation and what to say.

PRAYER Lord, it can be tricky to hold my tongue, especially when I get angry or upset. Instead of saying something I'll regret, I want to learn how to choose my words carefully.

DAY 60

My son, do not despise the Lord's discipline, and do not resent his rebuke, because the Lord disciplines those he loves, as a father the son he delights in.

–PROVERBS 3:11–12

Imagine you're watching your little cousin ride his tricycle when, suddenly, he takes off for the street. You stop him, but he pedals furiously toward the road again. A car is coming, so you make a decision. "Let's play out back," you announce. You grab a screaming toddler in one arm and his tricycle in the other.

Think about your cousin's perspective. He was having fun. But now, thanks to you, he's not. No wonder he's upset! "Yeah, but I knew better!" you would say. "I could see what was coming, and it wasn't good."

God, our heavenly Father, sees the oncoming "cars" in our lives, like negative influences, bad attitudes, and habits. So he takes away our "trikes," often through our parents or other adults. He's not killing our fun; he loves us so much that he would rather see us upset for now than hurt in the long run.

PRAYER Jesus, getting disciplined is no fun, but I know you do it because you love me. Help me see through my temporary irritation and resentment to trust my parents and other adults who are looking out for me.

DAY 61

Say to wisdom, "You are my sister," and to insight,
"You are my relative."

–PROVERBS 7:4

God has a couple of new family members to introduce and make part of your life: wisdom and insight. Wisdom is like an awesome older sister; she'll stick with you. She'll hold you back when you're about to do something not-so-great. When you're unsure of what the best choice is—like what to do about a broken friendship or how to respond to a bully—wisdom will guide you. She's the perfect sibling—even your parents will love her!

When you know wisdom like a sister, you form a bond and others will begin to see a connection. Insight, which is like a favorite cousin, gets noticed. What you are known for begins to grow to include *knowing* the right thing and *doing* the right thing grows too. A lot of people like to be around wisdom and insight.

You can read all about them in the book of Proverbs.

PRAYER

Lord, it sounds like wisdom is as important as my family, and I need wisdom in my life. Teach me her ways and how to bring her into my family.

DAY 62

Choose my instruction instead of silver, knowledge rather than choice gold, for wisdom is more precious than rubies, and nothing you desire can compare with her.

–PROVERBS 8:10-11

King Solomon could have asked God for anything—wealth, the best chariots, respect from everyone in the land, a long life, the best girlfriend, or having the largest army. Instead, Solomon requested something completely priceless: wisdom. Based on God's words, wisdom is a rare gift that can't be bought or sold. It's more than knowing all the answers. It also includes experience, knowledge, and good judgment that comes through in your actions.

Wisdom usually only comes from living a long life and having many different experiences. You don't just get wisdom and store it in a drawer or stuff it in your backpack. Instead, you nurture it and God grows it throughout your life. As you gain wisdom, it'll show. Others will notice and admire you for it. It will remain with you in school, at different jobs you'll have, in friendships, and family.

Rubies are lovely and gold comes in handy, but nothing you could ever desire compares with wisdom.

PRAYER God, please start giving me wisdom and showing me how valuable it is. I will pay attention to your words and ways so that my wisdom and insight can grow.

DAY 63

Ephesians 4:23–24 has a message about a new, improved you.
Unscramble the tiles to reveal the message.

E S S	Y O	R I	O F	T H E	T O	D T	N E W
S N E	T O	E L	S E	C R E	D S	E O U	N T
O B	G O	N T	M A D	P U	D I	A N D	I N
G H T	B E	E N	A T E	H O	U R	T O	L F
H E	M I N	T I T	R U E	U D E	S S	E W	L I N
A N D	I K E	A T

T O	B E					

DAY 64

Who are some of the wisest people you know? They could be in the news, in your family, or in the Bible. What makes each one wise?

_____
_____
_____
_____
_____
_____

DAY 65

A gossip betrays a confidence, but a trustworthy person keeps a secret.

–PROVERBS 11:13

Imagine your best friend grabbing your arm. "I have to tell you something, but you have to promise to keep it a secret!" Don't you get excited? You're getting the inside scoop. You lean in close and wonder what it could be.

Everyone likes a good secret.

But what happens after your friend shares her big news? Can you keep it to yourself? Or do you want to grab the arm of the next person and say, "I have to tell you something, just promise to keep it a secret!"

Sharing a secret can feel exciting at the moment, but passing it on will hurt the person who told you in the first place. Plus it tarnishes the trust your friend has in telling you something confidential.

A good secret-keeper is hard to come by, but God calls us to do just that. Unless the secret involves something bad (like a friend is in trouble, and you need to let an adult know about it), do your best to be a good secret-keeper.

PRAYER

Lord, sometimes I hear a secret and I want to tell someone else. Help me to be trustworthy for my friends. I want to hold on to their secrets like I would want them to hold on to mine.

DAY 66

Fools find no pleasure in understanding but delight in airing their own opinions.

−PROVERBS 18:2

Can you rub your belly and pat your head at the same time? Can you draw the number six while making clockwise circles with one of your legs? Can you listen and talk at the same time?

A fool does her fair share of talking and then some. The problem is that while her mouth is chattering away, her ears cannot listen. While a person is talking, she isn't listening, slowing down to understand, or gaining wisdom. She stays a fool. Her focus is on herself. She likes to give her opinion regardless of facts. And she doesn't catch on that she remains the biggest fan of her own voice.

On the other hand, the wise person seeks to understand before she talks. Her focus is on others. She realize she doesn't know everything about everything and can get more from listening than giving an opinion.

How much time will you spend closing your mouth and opening your ears?

PRAYER

Lord, there is no wisdom apart from you. I want to listen and recognize the words of the wise. Please lead me.

DAY 67

*A person's wisdom yields patience; it is to one's glory
to overlook an offense.*

–PROVERBS 19:11

Humans are wired with a strong sense of what is right and wrong. We also know what belongs to us. That's why babies' first words often are "no" and "mine!" It goes against human nature to ignore something that is being done to you or taken away. We want things to be fair!

So what was the writer trying to say in Proverbs 19:11? Think about the one who forgives an entire world. Instead of demanding that we get what we deserve, God patiently forgives us through his Son.

This verse doesn't mean you let yourself get bullied or be best friends with a person who is unkind to you. It does mean you should try to do your best at being slow to anger. Be quick to forgive and try being generous even when differences are obvious.

So what should you do when a classmate leaves you off her birthday party list? Overlook it; she could have forgotten or had to limit numbers. How should you react when your brother calls you a mean name? Swallow your anger and explain how it hurts your feelings.

When you model grace, you cause others to be curious about the God who does the same. There is more to life than being right, and that's showing Jesus to the world.

PRAYER I know wounds and annoying things are part of life. I'm going to start bringing them to you, Lord, so that I can handle them wisely. I want to point others toward you and your love rather than getting hung up on being right.

DAY 68

Gold there is, and rubies in abundance, but lips that speak knowledge are a rare jewel.

–PROVERBS 20:15

Rubies, deep red transparent gems, have been the most valuable jewel for centuries. They are rarer than diamonds and even more expensive. Rubies are only mined in a few places: Southeast Asia, a small portion of Africa, and some spots in the Middle East.

As rare as a ruby is—and who wouldn't want to own one of the most valuable jewels in the world?—there is something even better. Intelligent, wise words—they are more rare than rubies.

Think about all the words you speak every day. How many would compare to a rare jewel? Good words are very hard to find. But not impossible.

Wisdom, which comes from God, is the starting place for where we can find the most valuable words. Dig into your Bible and when you find a jewel, tuck it away in your heart. It will add value to your friendships. It will make your soul sparkle. Soon your life will be filled just like the best jewelry store on the planet.

PRAYER Lord, so many of my words come from my own ideas and thoughts. The more that come from you, the more valuable they will be. May I find your wisdom and keep it in my heart.

DAY 69

*If someone curses their father or mother, their lamp
will be snuffed out in pitch darkness.*

—PROVERBS 20:20

Baby eagles are clueless. To teach them to fly, their moms actually push them out of the nest. One by one, each eaglet flails wildly as it careens toward the ground. At the last second, the mother swoops under her baby and recues it. This routine repeats itself until every one of the baby eagles learns to fly by itself.

What would happen if one eaglet freaked out? "Are you crazy?" it might ask its mom. "I think I'll fly my own way." That rebel eagle wouldn't last long.

We have a lot in common with eagles. Even though a scurrying mouse isn't our idea of fast food, human parents sometimes push their children "out of the nest," or out of a comfort zone so that the kids will grow and figure out how to "fly."

Earthly parents aren't perfect—even when they are Christians. And you don't have to like everything your parents do. But God asks you to use your words, actions, and body language to honor Mom and Dad. After all, no one wants you to crash to the ground!

PRAYER God, it's hard to obey my mom or dad when we disagree. Please remind me they love me and are doing their best. Will you help me control my temper and show them my respect?

DAY 70

Starting at the arrow, go around the circle to the right. Write every other letter in the spaces provided to find out what Revelation 21:5a says.

__ ___ ___ _____ __

___ _____ _____," "_ __

_____ _____ ___."

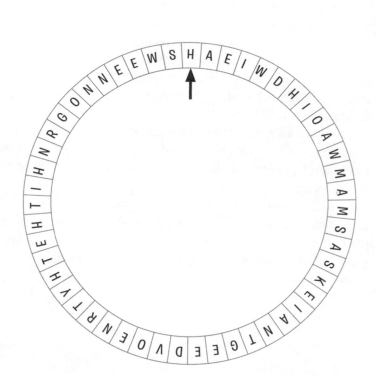

DAY 71

If I have children of my own someday I'll remember not to:

_____

_____

_____

_____

_____

_____

DAY 72

Fools give full vent to their rage, but the wise bring calm in the end.

–PROVERBS 29:11

One song I learned in Sunday school compares the foolish man to the wise man. The song was based on Jesus' sermon found in Matthew 7. The foolish man built his house on sand while the wise man built his house on rock. In both cases, a heavy rainstorm tested the strength of the buildings. The foolish man's house went flat, while the wise man's house stood firm.

The ways foolish people and wise people respond to upsetting circumstances in life result in different consequences. Fools don't take the time to think through what's going on. They lash out at the people who have upset them. But wise people make a smarter choice.

A wise person spends time building a deep relationship and sets a solid foundation based on honesty. The wise person takes time to think through a situation and figures out why they are upset before saying anything. She chooses to respond calmly. When all is said and done, fools let their storms rage and wash away friendships. But the wise will stand with friends and build an even stronger foundation.

PRAYER Lord, I've heard people talk foolishly. It's not peaceful or beautiful. Please help me respond wisely.

DAY 73

Out in the sea she will become a place to spread fishnets, for I have spoken, declares the Sovereign LORD. She will become plunder for the nations, and her settlements on the mainland will be ravaged by the sword. Then they will know that I am the LORD.

-EZEKIEL 26:5-6

Tyre was a beautiful seaside city that had two harbors. Most cities just have one. Not only can harbor cities defend themselves more easily, but their position on the water meant they owned or controlled trade routes. It was pretty simple to supply their city with everything they could need or want. They were self-sufficient, bustling, wealthy, and safe. Because of this powerful position, the people of Tyre gloated with pride and no longer turned to God.

But God Most High reminded Tyre that no one is above his judgment—or his love. Even mighty Tyre can be reduced to rubble, God forewarned. This was their chance to take him at his word, repent, and get to know him better. Instead they trusted in their own power and refused God's invitation.

Even today the most remarkable thing about Tyre is the rubble where fishnets are spread. Just like God said would happen if they didn't return to him.

PRAYER Lord, I accept your invitation to know you more. Please don't let my pride keep me from a real relationship with you.

DAY 74

"Cursed is the cheat who has an acceptable male in his flock and vows to give it, but then sacrifices a blemished animal to the Lord. For I am a great king," says the Lord Almighty, "and my name is to be feared among the nations."

—MALACHI 1:14

One of your best friends is having a birthday party, and you want to give her a beautiful expensive necklace.

Then you spot the most amazing shoes at the mall. So you wrap up some earrings you never liked instead of buying that necklace.

The "leftover" gift wouldn't mean much, would it? It didn't cost you money, effort, or brainpower. Whereas the necklace would have come from your heart.

Sometimes people give what they've got left to God. We might start off promising him our finest. Then we get tired, bored, or distracted and forget about our pledge.

In biblical times the Israelites showed their devotion to God by sacrificing their best farm animals. So when someone pretended to give a perfect animal but actually put a sick, small, or old creature on the altar, it disappointed God and actually made him sad.

God doesn't want our old, used stuff. Like a close friend, he wants us to trust him with everything we can possibly offer!

PRAYER God, I want to give you my best. When I'm half-hearted, I want to remember the ultimate sacrifice you made for me.

DAY 75

*Taking the five loaves and the two fish and looking up
to heaven, he gave thanks and broke the loaves. Then
he gave them to the disciples, and the disciples gave
them to the people. They all ate and were satisfied,
and the disciples picked up twelve basketsful of
broken pieces that were left over.*

–MATTHEW 14:19-20

Jesus gave thanks to the Father and then quietly performed a miracle that showed how much he cared and how different he was from other human beings. The disciples had front row seats and it was astonishing. It wasn't the first miracle they saw Jesus do, and it wouldn't be the last, but still this miracle surely helped them believe Jesus was the Son of God.

Even though they had faith, the disciples did not understand everything about Jesus and his plan. They expected Jesus to rule on earth, not die on the cross. They expected Jesus to save their nation like a king, not save the world through death. All of their expectations were turned upside down, and they spent a lot of time listening or asking questions.

But even when they didn't understand all the details of God's ways, they were changed by Jesus. They stayed close to the Savior, witnessed miracles, and believed.

PRAYER

Jesus, I'm glad the Bible records some of the amazing things you did, because I can have a front row seat to your power and love. Help me translate the awe and wonder into wisdom.

DAY 76

But the things that come out of a person's mouth come from the heart, and these defile them.

–MATTHEW 15:18

Don't ever tell a 1-year-old child to eat a worm. Why? Because he will! As babies start to crawl and walk, they learn about the world by sticking things in their mouths—no matter how dirty. Jesus said that a mouthful of worms, dirt, bugs, or germs isn't enough to earn the name of "unclean." Instead, Jesus taught that what is in the heart and mind can make people "unclean."

In Jesus' day, the Pharisees were the rock stars of the church. They knew every law by heart, could quote entire books of the Bible, and prided themselves on how "holy" they were because they followed the rules. Jesus, however, saw things differently. He knew that washing your hands before eating couldn't save your soul. The Pharisees judged others, lied, wished their annoying cousin would go away forever, and really wanted to own all of their neighbor's camels. In other words, the sin inside their hearts made them "unclean."

That's still true today. You might go to church camp or youth group and know dozens of Bible verses, but Jesus is most concerned about what's inside of you. Are you giving that proper attention?

PRAYER God, it's easy to hide behind all the rules I keep, but being "perfect" on the outside doesn't please you. I want my heart to please you as much as my actions.

DAY 77

Search up, down, and sideways to find the bolded words in the verse below.

For it is we **who are the circumcision**, we who **serve** God by **his Spirit**, who **boast** in **Christ Jesus**, **and** who **put** no **confidence** in the **flesh**.

–PHILIPPIANS 3:3

```
W  K  E  H  I  S  E  O  E  M  G  C  D  T  X  V  A  Q
J  X  H  W  A  V  O  K  J  R  I  P  B  S  J  Q  Z  M
N  D  T  R  R  S  U  F  L  R  A  U  Q  I  U  I  V  Z
I  E  J  E  H  C  O  C  C  C  U  T  P  R  T  C  G  X
W  W  S  W  W  R  A  U  B  O  A  S  T  H  O  H  W  P
I  M  G  A  V  O  M  N  H  M  D  L  V  C  Z  J  O  D
O  P  I  T  N  C  D  M  B  V  J  S  V  F  M  D  P  B
Q  T  P  U  I  D  N  H  V  B  V  W  P  E  S  Z  K  N
P  R  O  S  P  A  Z  H  V  F  Q  P  F  H  C  P  Q  H
P  R  I  U  X  J  U  I  I  B  H  Z  A  D  T  C  O  Z
X  O  Q  F  S  F  E  P  W  F  L  A  O  I  P  C  X  C
N  H  L  V  E  Z  X  S  E  R  T  V  J  B  H  N  V  K
H  R  H  H  H  C  G  C  U  V  M  I  W  V  Q  Q  J  B
N  G  R  W  H  T  Z  V  D  S  G  U  R  P  X  F  F  G
G  E  A  K  I  M  T  O  M  O  R  R  G  I  X  L  V  F
A  T  F  E  W  F  G  F  J  A  V  K  F  R  P  E  K  G
V  U  H  A  S  E  C  N  E  D  I  F  N  O  C  S  N  N
L  E  I  T  U  F  C  V  G  C  S  M  O  O  N  H  U  S
```

AND	FLESH	SERVE
ARE	FOR	SPIRIT
BOAST	GOD	THE
CHRIST	HIS	WHO
CIRCUMCISION	JESUS	
CONFIDENCE	PUT	

DAY 78

Write three questions you would ask Jesus if he was sitting next to you right now.

_____

_____

_____

_____

_____

_____

DAY 79

Everything they do is done for people to see: . . .
they love the place of honor at banquets and the most
important seats in the synagogues; they love to be
greeted with respect in the marketplaces and to be
called 'Rabbi' by others. . . . You blind guides! You
strain out a gnat but swallow a camel.

–MATTHEW 23:5-7, 24

The teachers of Jesus' day were focusing on stuff that didn't matter. In the process, they got puffed up, proud, and a little too full of themselves. They boasted about how much they knew God and then kind of forgot about him. They worked really hard to be know-it-alls.

The message Jesus brought to the leaders was that they were so focused on a tiny benefit for themselves that they missed the huge problem right in front of them. It was as though they didn't see a camel sitting in their food. Pride crept in and the teachers who were supposed to be helping other started to think how "great" they were. Sometimes it can become easy to forget what's important, but watch out for those camels. You don't want to accidentally swallow one!

PRAYER Lord, sometimes I get distracted by shallow things. I need you so I don't let those things go to my head and puff it up.

DAY 80

"What do you want me to do for you?" Jesus asked him. The blind man said, "Rabbi, I want to see." "Go," said Jesus, "your faith has healed you." Immediately he received his sight and followed Jesus along the road.

–MARK 10:51–52

Blind Bartimaeus spent his life in the dark. He couldn't see so he couldn't work. He was left on the side of the road, begging for any money people would give him. He had no hope that anything would change . . . until Jesus came near.

Bartimaeus was attracted to the Light of the World. When he heard Jesus was walking by, he made his faith known. "Jesus, Son of David, have mercy on me!" he shouted into the crowd. The crowd told him to be quiet, but he shouted more, "Son of David, have mercy on me!"

While the crowd tried to shush the embarrassing calls from a blind man, Jesus heard him and stopped. He gave the blind beggar his full attention and compassion. From that moment on, Bartimaeus was changed. Because of his faith, because of Jesus, the blind man could see. Instead of begging for mercy from the crowd, he was free to follow Jesus. And so he did.

PRAYER Lord, I want to see you. Give me the faith that blind Bartimaeus had. Change me and my heart so I can follow you.

DAY 81

Why do you look at the speck of sawdust in your brother's eye and pay no attention to the plank in your own eye? How can you say to your brother, 'Brother, let me take the speck out of your eye,' when you yourself fail to see the plank in your own eye?"

–LUKE 6:41-42

Imagine your friend looks across the lunch table at you. Cheese is hanging from your lip but you don't know it. Your friend starts laughing and pointing at the mess. "What?" you ask as you touch your face. When you finally feel the cheese goo, you wipe it off and say, "At least I don't have a big spot of spaghetti sauce on my chin!"

Jesus gave a whole lesson on pointing out others' messes. He knew how humans liked to criticize each other. See something negative and sure enough someone will point it out, make fun of it, or correct it. But that's not the smartest approach, especially if it turns out you might have a very noticeable flaw yourself! Check yourself first. Keep in mind Jesus knows all the flaws of every person. Rather than picking on somebody else's "low points," be understanding. You never know, it could turn out that you need the help.

PRAYER Jesus, I make mistakes, but you forgive me and wipe them away. I need that kind of grace when others mess up or get into their own problems.

DAY 82

Very truly I tell you, unless a kernel of wheat falls to
the ground and dies, it remains only a single seed. But
if it dies, it produces many seeds.

—JOHN 12:24

There's not much to a seed. Small and plain, it doesn't look that impressive. But when a seed is buried in the ground, a small miracle happens. It cracks open and becomes what it's really made for—something big and full. Seeds can become food that sustains life or flowers that color the world.

In this verse, Jesus is saying people are like seeds because we're made for something more. Our own plans and dreams leave us as small and plain as a seed. But if we follow Jesus and trust God to work in our lives, we will be part of his plan for something big, full, and abundant.

It's hard to imagine what beauty can come from a little seed like you or me, but God knows.

PRAYER Lord, I trust you and know you have great plans for me. I will keep praying and learning about you, so that I can grow into what you have designed for me.

DAY 83

You, therefore, have no excuse, you who pass judgment on someone else, for at whatever point you judge another, you are condemning yourself, because you who pass judgment do the same things.

–ROMANS 2:1

You see a classmate sneak a peek at someone else's test and you wonder if she'll get caught. Another "borrows" a really cool hoodie later in the day but never returns it, and you wonder if the one who took it will ever return it to the rightful owner. It's easy to spot others doing something wrong. We are even faster to notice when a Christian makes a bad choice.

So imagine how easy it is for others to notice *your* poor choices and mistakes. When I reverse the scenario, I start to wonder what I've done but didn't really notice. In the letter that Paul wrote to the Romans, he was saying, "Hey, be careful. If you start acting snooty and looking down your nose at others, they'll do exactly the same thing to you! And imagine what God thinks of the whole scenario!"

It makes sense for each of us to slow down and think twice about passing judgment. The next time we feel tempted to point out someone's faults, let's ask God to help us do the right thing in love.

PRAYER Lord, please help me catch myself when I start thinking bad thoughts about someone else. Help me examine my life and keep me humble.

DAY 84

Use the key to crack the code and find out why you might want to pray Psalm 51:10.

CREATE IN ME A CLEAN

HEART, O GOD,

AND RENEW A STEADFAST

SPIRIT WITHIN ME.

A = ✌

C = 👍

D = ♎

E = 👉

F = ☞

G = 👆

H = 〰

I = ✋

L = ●

M = ○

N = ■

O = 🏳

P = 🚩

R = ☼

S = 💧

T = ❄

W = ◆

DAY 85

What things happening in your life right now are making you upset? Write your list and then pray for God to help you see clearly what you should do or what you can change to improve these situations.

_____

_____

_____

_____

THE LORD'S WORD IS FLAWLESS: HE SHIELDS ALL WHO TAKE REFUGE IN HIM.
2 SAMUEL 22:31

DAY 86

We were therefore buried with him through baptism into death in order that, just as Christ was raised from the dead through the glory of the Father, we too may live a new life. For if we have been united with him in a death like his, we will certainly also be united with him in a resurrection like his.

–ROMANS 6:4-5

How can someone be alive but dead? How can someone be buried but resurrected? What kind of riddle is this? Since Paul was writing to a group of very smart people, he used a riddle to get their attention and make them think it through.

When God becomes part of your life, he changes the way you see the world and yourself so it is like sin dies and the bitterness of the world changes into joy for God's goodness; sin and the bad things of life won't have the same power over you. Your life is new, and it's like coming back from the dead.

Though it may still be tough to understand, God gives wisdom and the truth of his power is for everyone. Romans is a great book of the Bible to read and re-read all throughout life because there is so much to unravel and understand in God's Word.

PRAYER Lord, I want to see the world and the people around me the way you see them. Thank you for the resurrection of Jesus Christ and the changes he brings to my life.

DAY 87

What then? Shall we sin because we are not under the law but under grace? By no means!

–ROMANS 6:15

Laws were very important to the Jewish nation. They had laws about everything. So when Jesus offered grace and mercy, it was radical. Just one example is that people didn't have to sacrifice animals anymore; Jesus became that perfect, everlasting sacrifice, covering sins and providing a direct route to God.

When the rules change, it takes some time to figure out the "new rules." So for anyone who decided to follow Jesus, figuring out this new way of relating to God was tricky. For instance, if people weren't living by the Jewish laws anymore and pleasing God depended on your heart and mind instead of keeping every rule, was sinning such a big deal? Since people were covered by Jesus' blood, could they do whatever they felt like doing whenever they felt like doing it?

Paul's answer: No! When we sin, we become "slaves" to that sin. It runs our lives and drags us down. When Jesus sets us free from our sin, we feel so thankful that we should never want to do it again.

Think of it like this: If a fireman saves you from a burning building, would you say, "Thanks! I can't wait to start another fire with matches and gas as long as you're here to save me"?

PRAYER Jesus, thanks for taking away my guilt. Forgive me for treating that gift like it's no big deal. Please replace my desire to live for myself with a hunger to know you more.

DAY 88

For I have the desire to do what is good, but I cannot carry it out. For I do not do the good I want to do, but the evil I do not want to do—this I keep on doing.

—ROMANS 7:18-19

Paul readily admitted that he *planned* to do good but couldn't seem to pull it off.

Paul isn't the only one who faces this dilemma—we all do and that's why he wrote about it. We know what God expects of us. We agree that what he wants is a good thing. We don't want to lie, disobey, or fight with others. We know that kind of behavior gets everybody down, including our Creator. But we can't seem to resist the urges that pull us in that direction.

Guess what? That's exactly what the Lord is hoping we'll say. Until we see ourselves as hopeless in the fight against sin, we won't be interested in asking him to take over and save us. But once we see that we need what we don't have—his strength—we are willing to admit our sinfulness and accept Jesus' forgiveness and power. When the Holy Spirit comes into our hearts, the guilt of past failures goes away, and he gives us the ability to actually do what doesn't come naturally.

PRAYER Lord, I'm glad your Holy Spirit does what I can't do on my own. Thank you for your awesome power.

DAY 89

The mind governed by the flesh is death, but the mind governed by the Spirit is life and peace.

–ROMANS 8:6

What if you had a friend who only thought of herself? When you played together, she made up her own rules. She listened . . . but only to herself. She served cookies . . . to herself. She invited you over but then went in a room and closed the door to keep company . . . with herself. You probably wouldn't be friends for very long. That friendship would end.

When my mind is like a selfish friend and only focused on *itself*, the same result will happen. My selfishness will cause me to be by myself. When I only ask myself, "What is good *for me* right now?" there will be no relationships with other people.

But there's a different way. Instead of wrapping up in ourselves, we can wrap up in God. His way is all about loving him and loving others more than just loving ourselves. God assures us that sometimes it's hard to do, but it leads to life and peace. Considering others is not always convenient or super easy, but it's the life-giving way.

Naturally, we are all very selfish. Ultimately that leads to loneliness, sadness, and feeling unfulfilled. But God offers a different way that leads to life and peace inside and out.

PRAYER Lord, life and peace sound so much better than loneliness and selfishness. Thanks for loving me enough to show me the way.

DAY 90

Be joyful in hope, patient in affliction, faithful in prayer.

—ROMANS 12:12

When you were a baby, your complete communication style included cooing and crying. Eventually you learned other sounds, words, and sentences, but it didn't happen overnight. You had some real growing up to do.

We grow up spiritually too. Before we read the Bible and knew Jesus, we crawled around whimpering and wailing to get our way. But as we grew, we could move past demanding what we wanted exactly when we wanted it.

When trouble came and life got hard, our old way was to freak out, complain, and worry. But God gives us a new way of looking at life—with joy, patience, and faithfulness. God gives us hope, so we can trust and maybe even be joyful in tough times. Because we have him, we can be patient when there's trouble.

PRAYER Lord, help me to remember that joy, patience, and faithfulness are part of my new language as a growing Christian. Help me grow stronger in each.

DAY 91

Fill in the answers below. Answers are among the 66 books of the Bible. Then fill in the highlighted letters that go with the numbers. When you are finished, you will find out what to focus on instead of people's differences.

1. The first book of the Bible means origin __ __ __ __ [S] __ __

2. Joshua, Judges, [R] __ __ __

3. Song of Songs is also called Song of __ __ [L] __ __ __ __

4. The first gospel is __ [A] __ __ __ __ __

5. The last book of the Bible is __ __ __ __ __ __ [T] __ __ __

6. The Israelites were set free from Egypt in __ __ __ [D] __ __

7. One of the two books named after a woman __ __ __ [H] __ __

8. The first book after the gospels describes the early church __ [C] __ __

9. This prophet gives the most complete prophecy of Christ [I] __ __ __ __ __

10. This disciple's name appears on four books of the New Testament __ __ __ [N]

Here there is no Gentile or Jew, circumcised or uncircumcised, barbarian, Scythian, slave or free, but . . .

–COLOSSIANS 3:11

___ ___ ___ ___ ___ ___ ___ ___ ___ ___ ___, ___ ___ ___ ___ ___ ___ ___ ___ ___ ___ ___
 8 7 2 9 1 5   9 1   4 3 3   4 10 6   9 1   9 10   4 3 3

DAY 92

Happy words like HOPE and LOVE are important to keep in the front of your mind and even posted on the space around you (in your room, in your locker, on the fridge). Write down words that are positive and make you smile. Think about how you can keep these words in front of you throughout each day.

_____

_____

_____

_____

_____

_____

DAY 93

Will not the ministry of the Spirit be even more glorious?

−2 CORINTHIANS 3:8

If life is a great adventure, how are you going to travel? You can go it alone or you can follow the One who knows the way. You can stumble along or you can follow the One with the map, who knows where all the treasures lie.

If you decide to go solo, you risk missing a turn, losing your way, or getting too far down the wrong path. You might seek out shortcuts or stop in dangerous places. Your other choice is to take your quest with the Holy Spirit as the perfect guide. He sees around corners you can't. He's aware of all the best places to rest and the best times to push on. He knows all the supplies you'll need on the way.

So what kind of adventures will you go on in your life? God has big plans just for you, with your extraordinary and personal gifts and talents in mind. You can be assured that it's going to be a glorious adventure. You just have to trust your guide.

PRAYER Lord, sometimes I think my way is going to be best. I like my plans, my way. But I know your plans are greater, more exciting, more fulfilling. I choose to follow you.

DAY 94

Therefore, if anyone is in Christ, the new creation has come: The old has gone, the new is here!

—2 CORINTHIANS 5:17

The first time you saw a caterpillar, maybe you noticed its stumpy legs, or its bright colors, fuzzy outside, or tube-like body. Looking at those funny, beautiful, bizarre creepy-crawlies who would ever guess that they're different from other bugs or animals? That they change into something completely different? They don't just grow up like tadpoles grow into frogs. They changes into something completely *new*.

As a caterpillar, it crawls along the ground, but as a butterfly it flies. It used to plod along slowly, but now it swoops in the air. It used to gaze at the bottom of flowers, but now it sees thing from above. The transformation is complete and amazing.

This is what Paul is telling us in the verse. Accepting Christ holds the same transforming power of a caterpillar turning into a butterfly. You don't sprout wings, but you start seeing things from above, from his viewpoint. Your beauty grows from the inside out. You're still you, but are moving into a lighter, freer you. It doesn't happen overnight. It's a process. But the transformation to something completely new is promised.

PRAYER I can't imagine how it feels to change from a caterpillar into a butterfly. I'm excited because you promise to transform me in beautiful ways. Since it's in your hands, Lord, I know it's going to be awesome.

DAY 95

When I saw that they were not acting in line with the truth of the gospel, I said to Cephas in front of them all, "You are a Jew, yet you live like a Gentile and not like a Jew. How is it, then, that you force Gentiles to follow Jewish customs?"

—GALATIANS 2:14

Quick history lesson: The Jews followed certain strict rules. Because they honored these laws, many Jews wouldn't eat with or hang out with people unless they were also following the rules. When Jesus came to earth, he became our salvation—following the rules wasn't the way to salvation any longer. That meant Gentiles could be saved too.

Peter knew Jews and Gentiles were saved by Jesus. But when some super strict Jews visited, Peter began pulling away from his Gentile buddies, afraid of what the Jews might say or think. So Paul called him out on it.

Sometimes we are like Peter, wondering what others think instead of trusting what God says. Other times we are like Paul, trying to lovingly point out where a friend might be missing the mark.

Paul didn't want to be right; he just wanted everyone to know and love Jesus. Peter had the same goal but temporarily lost sight of it. The key? Not caring about who "wins" an argument but remembering God's message of love.

PRAYER

Lord, help me be courageous but loving, concerned only about honoring you. And when someone confronts me, teach me to accept that correction with humility and wisdom.

DAY 96

*I have been crucified with Christ and I no longer live,
but Christ lives in me. The life I now live in the body, I
live by faith in the Son of God, who loved me and gave
himself for me.*

—GALATIANS 2:20

Queens are not elected like presidents. They sit on their throne for as long as they live. Only when they die does a new king or queen take over.

We are like queens in the world of our hearts. We rule as our own highest authority. We decide everything—what we spend time doing, what things we want to have, the thoughts we dwell on, and the list goes on. There's no room for another ruler until death. So God says, "That heart queen needs to die, so I can step in and sit on the throne of your heart."

In the letter to the Galatians, Paul said, "Jesus rules in my life. He died on the cross for me. So I took my selfish ways and put them on the cross too. I want Christ to rule in my heart."

You can follow the King of kings too. Invite Jesus on the throne of your heart. Share all your thoughts, feelings, and fears with him. He will draw you near not just as a ruler but as a loving friend.

PRAYER Lord, I invite you to take over my heart. I want you to lead me and draw me close.

DAY 97

. . . I warn you, as I did before, that those who live like this will not inherit the kingdom of God.

–GALATIANS 5:21

The apostle Paul says, "The acts of the flesh are obvious." That is, the way we act is for everyone to see and know. Our hearts and minds are naturally selfish (wanting what is best for me), negative (you aren't as good as her), jealous (I wish I had that), and sometimes hateful (she doesn't deserve that). Because our thoughts and attitudes are naturally sinful, our separation from God is natural too. Sometimes we ignore him and battle for what we think is best. Sometimes we even have fits of rage and argue with others.

Thankfully the Holy Spirit sets us free from destructive ways, so we can inherit the kingdom of God. We move toward considering others and loving them as ourselves, sharing, cooperating and working together. As soon as we accept Jesus' message of love, we see and learn better ways, specifically how to love God and others. We begin to inherit the kingdom of God through love.

And that's reason to celebrate.

PRAYER

Lord, help me see what you see and cooperate with the Holy Spirit. I'm grateful to be changed.

DAY 98

Practice your coin counting to complete the puzzle. When you're done, you'll find out Jesus' important message.

Jesus replied, "Very truly I tell you, ___ _____
                                        (2 dimes) (8 nickels)

_____ _____ _____ _____ ____ _____
(2 quarters) (2 dimes (20 pennies)   (4 quarters)   (2 nickels) (10 dimes)
             +1 nickel)

_____ _____ _____ _____ _____."
(5 nickels)   (1 dime)   (10 pennies) (10 nickels)   (4 dimes)

-John 3:3

10	20	25	40	50	100
of	no	see	one	can	God
are	the	unless	again	born	kingdom
they					

DAY 99

The kingdom of God is filled with:

_____

_____

_____

_____

_____

_____

DAY 100

*But now you must also rid yourselves of all such
things as these: anger, rage, malice, slander, and filthy
language from your lips . . . Therefore, as God's chosen
people, holy and dearly loved, clothe yourselves
with compassion, kindness, humility, gentleness and
patience.*

—COLOSSIANS 3:8, 12

You've heard the phrase, "Garbage in, garbage out." Garbage inside you doesn't just stay tucked away. It spills out.

Biting words, bad-mouthing, gossiping—this kind of speaking isn't just harmless expression. It comes from somewhere. If someone has been angry at her mom for weeks but never said a word, that anger is brewing inside. If it brews too long, it will bubble up in hurtful words.

It also works this way: If you watch lots of shows with backbiting characters, the garbage gets absorbed by your brain. Sooner or later, those words will be peppering your own speech. Garbage coming out of your mouth means there was garbage inside, like one, big trash recycling fest.

The way to get rid of the garbage? Load up with God's Word, love, and goodness. Then kind words, gentleness, and compassion will fill you inside and flow out.

PRAYER

Lord, I should have control over my own mouth even if I hear lots of nastiness around me. I need wisdom to put goodness into my soul more than the garbage.

DAY 101

We hear that some among you are idle and disruptive.
They are not busy; they are busybodies. Such people
we command and urge in the Lord Jesus Christ to
settle down and earn the food they eat.

–2 THESSALONIANS 3:11–12

There are friendly questions: "How are you?" "Did you like the concert last night?" "That math homework was hard, didn't you think?" And there are busybody questions: "What were you talking to her about?" "What did the teacher give him?" "Is that your journal? What's it say?"

A busybody meddles in other people's business. She wants to know the scoop on everyone. She inserts herself into situations that don't involve her at all. She buzzes around from person to person but with little purpose except to be in the know. Curious and careless, busybodies start rumors.

It's natural to be curious and want to share opinions. That doesn't make you a busybody. If you pry too much or pipe up too often, stop to ask yourself why. Are you satisfying your own curiosity or genuinely caring about a friend? Focus first on taking care of your own business. Then you'll find you have less time to worry about someone else's.

PRAYER

Lord, I don't think I'm a busybody, but I definitely let my curiosity take over at times. Help me to see where that fine line is between care and curiosity.

DAY 102

*The words "once more" indicate the removing of what
can be shaken—that is, created things—so that what
cannot be shaken may remain.*

–HEBREWS 12:27

When a house burns to the ground, there is still some chance that things of value could have survived. So home owners might sift through the ashes using a box with a screen at the bottom. They scoop up ashes in the box and then shake it back and forth. The ash falls through the grate, leaving behind bigger, more valuable pieces, like china, jewelry, and heirlooms.

This verse encourages shaking the ash away from the things that are most important in our lives. Only God's Word and people are eternal. Nothing else lasts. Instead of counting on things that are temporary or relying on things that fall away, we build a relationship with the living God. We build up a faith that can't be shaken by circumstances. Everything else can fall away like ash.

Your faith can be built up strong because it is based on a powerful, eternal, good God. Then when things shake and rattle and ash falls through the grate, you'll be left with what matters.

PRAYER

Lord, help me see when I am distracted by things that can be shaken instead of relying on you. I want a close relationship with you and a strong faith. With you, I am unshakable.

DAY 103

Likewise, the tongue is a small part of the body, but it makes great boasts. Consider what a great forest is set on fire by a small spark.

–JAMES 3:5

When you were younger did you ever get in trouble for sticking out your tongue? If you couldn't find the way to say something cutting, sticking out your tongue could say how you felt.

Even now, your tongue can be a concealed weapon. With it, you are capable of defending yourself or another. But that little muscle in your mouth is also lethal. It can kill someone's reputation or wound a person's spirit. Quite possibly you have been injured by someone else's tongue. This verse reminds us that the tongue is like a spark that starts a forest fire.

That's why we have to be careful with what we say, especially when we are angry or hurt. Words can fly fast and furious from our mouths before we have time to think about what we are saying. And once the words are out, you can't take them back.

As followers of Jesus, we need to watch our words. Those who know we're Christians will draw conclusions about God based on what rolls off our tongues.

PRAYER Lord, my mouth belongs to you. Give me the wisdom to know when to open it and when to keep it shut.

DAY 104

I know your deeds, that you are neither cold nor hot. I wish you were either one or the other! So, because you are lukewarm—neither hot nor cold—I am about to spit you out of my mouth.

—REVELATION 3:15-16

You grab a mug of hot chocolate, but it's just lukewarm. Yuck! The Bible has something to say about being lukewarm Christians. But the Lord isn't talking about their physical temperature; he was referring to behavior.

The Laodiceans weren't God's enemies, but they weren't best friends either. And Jesus didn't like that: "I am about to spit you out of my mouth" (vs. 16).

If you'd rather not be spit out, ask yourself these questions:

- Do I attend church because I want to?
- Are my prayers filled with "Give me" and "I want"? Do I treat God like a magic genie in a bottle?
- Am I embarrassed to tell others I believe in Jesus?
- Is growing my faith important to me?

If your passion for Jesus has cooled, ask God to heat it up. With his help, your spiritual hot chocolate will soon be piping hot again.

PRAYER God, has my love for you grown cold? I didn't even realize it was happening. Please forgive me. Your love isn't halfway, so I don't want mine to be either!

I AM CHANGED

SECTION 3

Be His

Your love has made me see,

Only You could be the

miracle in me!

DAY 106

Where do you belong? What's your identity? Write what's on your heart.

DAY 107

You are my strength, I watch for you; you, God, are my fortress.

—PSALM 59:9

It's fun to play games that don't have a lot of rules or require a lot of equipment. Like the license plate game on a road trip. As you pass cars, you note the state they are from, trying find all fifty states. The alphabet game is another. From your seat, you try to find all twenty-six letters in the alphabet on road signs and billboards.

The next time you need a game to play, go on a God hunt. Look for indications that God has been at work in your daily life. Where has God left his fingerprints? What is something out of the ordinary that proves God is looking out for you? When something happens that points to God's love for you, write it down. Keep a log of your God sightings.

The psalmist says he watches for God. As he goes about his day, he keeps his eyes open for ways that his heavenly Father shows up. Because God has been faithful in the past, the psalmist knows to look for how God will be faithful again. No wonder he thinks of God as a fortress. The psalmist feels protected knowing that God is not far away.

PRAYER Lord, I will be on the lookout for you today. Give me the ability to see you working in my life and in my world.

DAY 108

My flesh and my heart may fail, but God is the strength of my heart and my portion forever.

–PSALM 73:26

When was the last time you were sick enough to stay home from school? Even a cold can make you feel lousy enough to stay inside, away from friends, and lay low until you feel better. Some illnesses linger for a long time or land on holidays, making it pretty hard to celebrate. When you get sick and the rest of your life goes on hold until you're back on your feet, it becomes easy to realize that health is very important.

But it's not the *most* important thing.

Our relationship with God ranks higher than health. God cares about our circumstances on earth (he is the Great Physician after all). But he also touches the deepest stirrings of our souls. He is the God of the physical and the eternal, our bodies and our hearts.

As great as the physical world is, it's not made for forever. It's a vapor compared to eternity. But until then, where we are weak, sick, or exhausted, God is enough.

PRAYER

Thank you for taking care of my body and soul, the temporary and the eternal. You are over everything. I am encouraged that you are all I need.

DAY 109

It is you alone who are to be feared. Who can stand before you when you are angry?

−PSALM 76:7

From the time we are little, we learn that God is loving. But he has many emotions besides love. Just like us, God can be sad, frustrated, and even angry.

Wait—the Lord can be both angry and loving? Sure. Think about your parents or a teacher. When you make a really bad decision, they don't react by smiling and saying, "Oh well." When you veer wildly off course, they get angry, not because they enjoy feeling mad, but because they want you to have the best life.

Similarly, God hates it when we sin, because as a perfect, sinless God, he can't stand to be around sin. That's why Jesus died; he acted as the flawless sacrifice to make a way for us to spend forever with our heavenly Father.

So does that mean we're stuck with a mean, grumpy God? No way! God gets angry at all the horrible things he sees in his universe—not because he hates us. In fact, he loves us like crazy and never wants to be separated from us. That's why he gets angry at all the things that try to separate us from him! The Lord is protective of his children and will display his anger whenever Satan tries to snatch one away.

PRAYER

Anger is scary, God, but I know your anger comes out of your love for me and your hatred of sin. Thank you for providing Jesus to cover my sins and bring me into your family.

DAY 110

As a father has compassion on his children, so the
LORD has compassion on those who fear him; for he
knows how we are formed, he remembers that we are
dust.

-PSALM 103:13, 14

God knows you inside and out—from your guts to your eyebrows. He doesn't shake his head and wonder, "What happened with that one? I thought I did a better job with her." He doesn't slap his forehead and say, "Wow. I didn't think she would make that mistake today. I'm shocked!"

God knows that you won't always make the right decision. He knows the world is corrupt, and sometimes you will slip up. He also knows that people can be mean and hurt your feelings. But just like a good dad is there for his kids, God is there for you. His heart is big, and his love is strong. Those things don't change based on what you do or what happens to you.

He knows all the decisions you make over your lifetime. He has already planned out how he will shape you and change you based on everything that happens over the years. He even knows how long you will live. And every day, he waits to show his compassion and grace to you.

PRAYER God, I need you. I need you when I mess up, and I need you when I'm hurt. Thank you for being a good dad.

DAY 111

For you created my inmost being; you knit me
together in my mother's womb. I praise you because
I am fearfully and wonderfully made; your works are
wonderful, I know that full well.

−PSALM 139:13-14

Even if God were just an artist, we would check out his art shows with wonder. Only a creative master could dream up the grace of a giraffe, the power of a volcano, the shine of the moon. The same artist who fashioned a sunflower also fashioned a rhino. The same potter who sculpted a peanut, designed a rainbow. There is just no end to his greatness and power.

In Genesis, God saved his best work for last: humans. He said, "Very good," when he looked at humans. We are created in God's image after all. The same one who formed our brains designed our hearts and dreamed up our souls. He painted our emotions and our smiles.

This verse above suggests that God's creation, his handiwork, his creativity, his participation happens all the time. It wasn't "one and done" when he set the world in motion. He personally had a hand in creating *you*. You are amazingly and marvelously made by the Master. You are a work of love!

PRAYER Everywhere I look, I see your fingerprints, Lord. It makes me appreciate things more, including the way you made me.

DAY 112

Search up, down, and sideways to find the bolded words in this verse from John.

Yet to **all who did receive him**, to **those** who **believed** in **his name**, he **gave the right** to **become children** of **God**.

−JOHN 1:12

```
R  A  D  Y  S  D  O  R  Q  E  X  P  D  Y  C  B  X  O
T  N  P  I  U  M  O  E  M  P  H  T  U  N  A  E  Y  C
T  Y  Q  B  D  X  O  G  V  V  S  L  R  T  L  D  K  I
J  E  U  Y  T  X  J  B  Y  A  U  I  Q  I  T  M  H  W
O  Z  G  I  V  S  U  N  T  N  G  V  B  O  I  A  X  Z
M  O  R  Z  P  W  X  X  L  B  H  O  M  D  Z  A  P  Q
D  Y  Z  T  K  K  T  D  B  I  K  E  E  S  H  X  B  Z
V  P  M  H  O  P  S  R  S  E  A  O  A  J  J  R  M  T
E  V  V  O  Q  A  I  W  A  K  C  Z  Q  D  E  B  Y  D
R  T  P  S  F  G  Q  N  J  K  E  O  T  E  I  B  X  Z
W  X  Y  E  H  R  E  C  E  I  V  E  M  V  Z  J  Y  J
N  A  U  T  C  R  A  Y  G  T  T  O  T  E  J  W  J  C
T  X  D  O  D  E  H  T  J  L  N  P  E  I  H  W  E  V
J  U  A  L  R  C  E  O  N  I  C  U  Y  L  I  S  G  C
B  N  I  W  H  O  C  Y  I  M  G  P  L  E  M  F  B  Q
C  H  B  I  N  O  N  V  T  Z  J  E  H  B  L  W  L  W
C  N  S  Q  O  C  E  M  A  N  A  R  U  L  K  K  Y  S
T  G  V  D  O  D  T  X  Y  A  F  N  A  I  H  G  X  U
```

ALL	GOD	THE
BECOME	HIM	THOSE
BELIEVED	HIS	WHO
CHILDREN	NAME	YET
DID	RECEIVE	
GAVE	RIGHT	

DAY 113

Write down at least ten things you like about yourself. God made you this way for a reason. You are amazing!

_____

_____

_____

_____

_____

_____

DAY 114

I cry aloud to the LORD; I lift up my voice to the LORD for mercy. I pour out before him my complaint; before him I tell my trouble.

−PSALM 142:1−2

Some days, everything happens easily and smoothly. Your teacher gives you praise, your dad gives you hugs, your mom gives you cookies, and your siblings give you smiles. And then there are days when nothing goes right. You forget your homework, your dad misses his flight home, your mom burns the cookies, and your siblings give you nothing but a hard time. These are the days when emotions bubble up and threaten to blow like a volcano. What do you do when all you feel like doing is pounding a pillow, shaking your fist, and stomping your feet?

You give it to God, because he can take it better than anyone. You can let it all out with him. He wants to hear your honest thoughts. He won't turn away from you. He won't tease you for how you feel.

He listens unfailingly. He understands completely. He already knows it anyway, so why not hash it out with him? Whatever is bothering you most, whatever is hurting you, whatever is making you mad, tell him like it is. He is safe.

PRAYER

Lord, I have so many feelings right now. I don't understand them all. I want to feel better. Show me what to do.

DAY 115

A good name is more desirable than great riches; to be esteemed is better than silver or gold.

–PROVERBS 22:1

A good name has nothing to do with how it's pronounced, how it's spelled, or how unique it is. What ultimately makes your name good or bad is what people think of when they hear it. Does your name give them good vibes or bad? Can they trust you? Do they like to spend time with you? Do they never tell you a secret? Do people wonder what you say behind their backs?

In one of William Shakespeare's plays called *Othello*, a soldier by the name of Iago gives a moving speech that celebrates the importance of having a good reputation. Iago says that being robbed of your name is worse than having your wallet stolen. In other words, you can always replace your purse, ID card, phone, lip gloss, and even cash, but once your name has been tarnished, you're toast.

Wise King Solomon said that being a person who keeps her word and is trustworthy is worth more than winning the lottery. For others to think highly of you is priceless. So how good is your name?

PRAYER Lord, with your help, I want to be a person others can trust. I want my name to bring a smile to their faces.

DAY 116

"My lover is mine and I am his; . . ."

–SONG OF SOLOMON 2:16A

It's true, there are different kinds of love. You don't love pizza the way you love your mom. Even the most diehard fans don't love the Seattle Seahawks the same way they love their children. The love you have for your grandma is different from the love you'll have for your husband.

The Bible paints a picture of the kind of love that we can share with the Lord. It's not easy describing this love with mere words when it involves a super huge, infinitely perfect God. "Friend," "lover," and "father" are all different relationships to describe a fuller, more complete picture of love between God and his people. Each one offers a different angle on intimacy.

Intimacy is knowing each other very well and being true to each other. In a word, it describes closeness, warmth, confidence, and attachment. All these good things are worth working for, but it may not always be easy. Any relationship can be messy with betrayal and misunderstanding. But God keeps encouraging us to "come to me." That's the best invitation you'll ever get.

PRAYER

Jesus, thank you for loving me and knowing me intimately. I want to know you with the same confidence and devotion. Thank you for your Word that shows me the truth of who you are. Thank you for a relationship with you that breathes life into me.

DAY 117

The LORD Almighty will come with thunder and earthquake and great noise, with windstorm and tempest and flames of a devouring fire.

−ISAIAH 29:6

Rain helps plants grow, but it can also wash away hillsides and destroy roads. Fire warms a house in winter and roasts marshmallows, but one spark can ignite a whole forest fire. Wind blows pollen from a flower and spreads seeds, but in a hurricane, it can knock down houses. How can nature be so gentle and yet so mighty?

The outdoor world reflects the nature of God. He is gentle and loving, but he is strong and powerful. He cares for the hurting and needy, but he will defeat evil with a mighty blow. Humans have no control over nature or over God. He can make it rain or stop the rain from flooding a river. He can put out a spark of fire or rain it down from heaven to consume a soaking wet altar. (See 1 Kings 18.)

Look outside today. What do you see or feel? A light breeze or the warmth of the sun—thank God for his gentle touch. A thunderstorm or blizzard—thank God for his mighty power that saves you and defeats the devil. Let nature show you the wonders of God.

PRAYER God, you are powerful and strong yet gentle and loving. That's amazing.

DAY 118

*But now, this is what the L*ORD *says—he who created you, Jacob, he who formed you, Israel: "Do not fear, for I have redeemed you; I have summoned you by name; you are mine."*

-ISAIAH 43:1

Have you ever seen the stadium where the Seattle Seahawks play football? It holds almost 70,000 people at one time. And yet, despite all the faces, all the numbers, the commotion of the crowd, God could stroll into the stadium, point to you, and call you by name. "I know you," he could say. "You are mine."

Sometimes God talks to Israel and an entire race of people. He reminds them that they have a special bond. Sometimes God speaks to the heart of an individual. And he reminds each person they have a special bond. He's big enough to embrace a whole nation—a whole world—and close enough to embrace a single human being.

God knows your name. You are not just a face in a crowd. You are individually known and specifically loved. All your talents? He knows them. All your fears? He knows them. He says, "I've got you. Don't be afraid."

How does it feel to get up in the morning knowing that your heart, your character, your name is known by the powerful and personal God?

PRAYER Lord, it's so great that you're not a distant God who leaves me alone, but you want a relationship with me. I am so glad to be yours.

DAY 119

Galatians 3:29 reveals who we are in Christ. Unscramble the tiles to reveal the whole message.

ARE	ED	LON	THE	IRS	O	C	RAH	N	Y
COR	HRI	E	YOU	OU	AND	ST		HE	
SE	IF	G T	PRO	BE	AMS	DIN	MIS		
G	THE	AC	O T	AB					

I F	Y O U						

DAY 120

When I look outside, I see God's handiwork in the world this way . . .

_____

_____

_____

_____

_____

_____

DAY 121

Then I said to the priests and all these people, "This is what the L̲o̲r̲d̲ says: Do not listen to the prophets who say, 'Very soon now the articles from the L̲o̲r̲d̲'s house will be brought back from Babylon.' They are prophesying lies to you."

–JEREMIAH 27:16

People don't always get things right. It happened a lot in the Bible. Some guys would say God said one thing. Then other guys would say God said something different. People would get confused. What did God *really* say?

We have to be careful. Just because someone says, "God told me that you are going to win that football game," doesn't mean it's true. In the Bible, they called those people *false prophets*. They would go around telling people that God wasn't mad when he was. Or they would say God was going to help them win a war, but God didn't even want them to go to war!

The best way to know for sure is to check the Bible, ask God yourself, and ask for guidance from godly adults. Sometimes all you need to do is to sit back and see if what a person said comes true. Time will always tell if someone was sharing a message from God or their own ideas.

PRAYER God, teach me to hear your voice. Show me how to be a good listener and to have good judgment about what other people say about you.

DAY 122

Jehonadab son of Rekab ordered his descendants not to drink wine and this command has been kept. To this day they do not drink wine, because they obey their forefather's command. But I have spoken to you again and again, yet you have not obeyed me.

–JEREMIAH 35:14

Jehonadab told his children and grandchildren not to drink wine. They listened. Even when they grew up, they never took a single sip. Then God looked at Israel. They didn't follow what God said. He told his people over and over what they needed to do. And every time, they didn't listen. It was frustrating because one group of people obeyed their granddad, while God's people didn't seem to hear a thing he said.

God doesn't ask for obedience just because. He wants people to obey him because he knows best. In the same way we listen to our parents, a teacher, or coach, God wants us to listen to him when he says, "Love me, love people, don't steal . . ."

When we choose to listen to God and obey the one who loves us most, he's delighted. And our lives are blessed.

PRAYER

Lord, I want to listen and obey. Help me to take my faith seriously and follow you.

DAY 123

Yet I will remember the covenant I made with you in the days of your youth, and I will establish an everlasting covenant with you.

–EZEKIEL 16:60

In women's international gymnastics, Russia and the USA often battle for the top spots. To make the team, a young girl must commit to hours of daily practice for many years. Only a few of the highest achievers can wear the national leotard and practice in an Olympic training center. So can you imagine if one of these gymnasts suddenly decided to quit their nation's team and join the other team?

Gymnasts are often more loyal to their teams than some humans are to the Lord. Take the Israelites for example. Even though God constantly loved, guided, and protected them, they often dumped him for other gods and even human kings!

Bad move. Out from under God's protection Israel lost battles, suffered droughts and famines, and were taken captive by ruthless nations. But if they weren't going to hold up their end of the deal and follow him, he wouldn't stop the consequences.

Thankfully, even when we abandon him, God waits for us to return. Don't break your own everlasting covenant with God. Stick with your first (and best) team. After all, he's the best coach ever.

PRAYER God, I've joined your team by giving my life to you. I want to represent your name and bring you honor by my performance.

DAY 124

*For the day is near, the day of the LORD is near—a
day of clouds, a time of doom for the nations. A sword
will come against Egypt, and anguish will come upon
Cush. When the slain fall in Egypt, her wealth will be
carried away and her foundations torn down.*

—EZEKIEL 30: 3-4

Ezekiel was always the bearer of bad news. Destruction here.
Death there. Drought, famine, and captivity. No wonder no
one wanted to listen to what Ezekiel had to say. How does all that
match up with a loving God? This is a big question that makes it
hard for people to follow God. But it's not that complicated.

God is completely good. He made the world and everything
in it. And he set up the way the world should run—based on his
goodness and truth. But he lets people choose whether they follow his rules. People (and nations) continue to ignore God's call to
trust him completely. It's their loss when they choose to live apart
from God and his best laid plans for a healthy and happy life. God
has great love for us, so great he lets us make the choice.

PRAYER

God, please help me understand how your love and
judgment go together rather than being a contradic-
tion. Then I can be ready to answer anyone who has
a hard time understanding them too.

DAY 125

"For this is what the Sovereign LORD says: I myself will search for my sheep and look after them. As a shepherd looks after his scattered flock when he is with them, so will I look after my sheep. I will rescue them from all the places where they were scattered on a day of clouds and darkness.

−EZEKIEL 34:11-12

What are sheep without a shepherd? Lost. And they won't make it too long on their own. Sheep depend on their shepherd for their very lives, because they're not equipped to defend themselves. They don't have sharp teeth to fight against predators, and they're not fast enough to escape. Plus sheep tend to wander, munching on grass without paying attention. When they look up, they realize they are away from the flock, apart from the shepherd, and sometime in a whole lot of trouble. Their only chance to come back to safety is to be found and rescued by the shepherd they know.

People are a lot like wandering sheep. We need the attention and protection of a shepherd who leads. Thankfully the sovereign Lord himself has volunteered for the role. He is the one we follow, whose voice we know, whose care we rely on. He lovingly says, "I myself will look after them. I will rescue them."

The Lord himself is looking after you. He can speak to you like no other shepherd. Learn to hear his voice and follow him.

PRAYER My Good Shepherd, thank you for caring even when I wander and get lost. You know me, and I want to know you too.

DAY 126

Write the words of the verse below in the crossword puzzle.
(Hint: Start with the longest word.)

. . . and giving joyful thanks to the Father, who has
qualified you to share in the inheritance of his holy
people in the kingdom of light.

—COLOSSIANS 1:12

DAY 127

Jesus is called the Good Shepherd. What other names of Jesus do you know from the Bible? What names would you give him?

_____

_____

_____

_____

_____

_____

Strength

SALVATION

LiGHt

GREaT

LOVE

DAY 128

The Lord your God is with you, the Mighty Warrior who saves. He will take great delight in you; in his love he will no longer rebuke you, but will rejoice over you with singing.

—ZEPHANIAH 3:17

If the nation of Israel had a middle name, it would be Fickle. Fickle means to change frequently, especially in regard to one's loyalties, interests, or affection.

Skimming through the Old Testament, you read about the Israelites going from good to bad, from following God to ditching him. Like a mixed up squirrel, they can't decide which way to run.

So God occasionally let Israel suffer the consequences. When the people weren't trusting him, for example, he allowed other nations to successfully attack them. Sometimes the Israelites came back to the Lord while other times they stubbornly kept resisting him. God knows when to punish and when to restore. He knew when Israel needed a Mighty Warrior to fight their battles.

Just like Israel, we flip-flop between obeying God and doing our own thing. Thankfully, in his wisdom, he sees what will and won't bring us to our senses. God fights for us, even when we're not perfect. Don't you think someone like that deserves our full-time allegiance and loyalty?

PRAYER Lord, I think I wrongly imagine you as a dictator who loves to punish me. But that's not right—your word says you take delight in me. Thanks for being my Mighty Warrior.

DAY 129

"Go to the village ahead of you, and just as you enter it, you will find a colt tied there, which no one has ever ridden. Untie it and bring it here. If anyone asks you, 'Why are you doing this?' say, 'The Lord needs it and will send it back here shortly.'"

–MARK 11: 2-3

Jesus gave some strange instructions to two of his disciples in those verses from Mark's gospel. They probably wondered if they heard him right.

In those days, when royalty traveled from town to town, they paraded in on horses. Horses represented war, military might, and power. Sounds like the perfect ride for a king, right? But Jesus put a twist on that tradition. Instead of presenting himself as an earthly and majestic ruler, he chose a donkey as his transportation. Donkeys, unlike horses, stood for peace—an even better choice for the Prince of Peace.

As the crowd cheered for Jesus, many probably thought of Zechariah 9:9: "See, your king comes to you, righteous and victorious, lowly and riding on a donkey, on a colt, the foal of a donkey." It was like a giant arrow pointing to Jesus saying, HERE IS YOUR KING!

Now you know why Jesus' strange orders make sense. Remember, every move the Lord makes is purposeful and meaningful. He won't steer you wrong.

PRAYER Jesus, you know everything. Yet sometimes I still question what you tell me to do. Please give me a heart that wants to obey you, even when your directions don't make sense to me.

DAY 130

*Do not be afraid, little flock, for your Father has been
pleased to give you the kingdom.*

–LUKE 12:32

This verse is full of tenderness from the Good Shepherd. It
reassures his children that they have the attention, care, and
love of a heavenly Father whose plan for them is all good. Valuing
joy, grace, compassion, and peace, he loves to spend time with
you. The Father is King, and you, sweet princess, are his.

Because you are his, you don't have to be afraid; you have
someone to trust. Because you are his, you don't have to worry
about your future; you have been promised the kingdom. Because
you are his, he is not only extravagantly generous with his love
but *pleased* about it. He doesn't give gifts because he's obligated
but because he's delighted.

If you are discouraged, anxious, or fearful about something,
remember the reassurance of this verse. Remember who you are,
but especially *whose* you are.

PRAYER
You have already given so much to me, Lord. Thank
you for speaking to my fear and worry and for being
my safe place. My comfort comes in knowing you
and trusting what you say. I remember who you are,
God, and that I am yours.

DAY 131

"If anyone comes to me and does not hate father and mother, wife and children, brothers and sisters—yes, even their own life—such a person cannot be my disciple."

–LUKE 14:26

Doesn't it seem strange that Jesus said people are supposed to hate their parents in order to follow him? After all, one of the Ten Commandments says to "honor your father and mother." Plus, Jesus came down pretty hard on some people who gave money to the temple instead of helping their older parents pay bills. This sounds confusing.

Now think about your mom and dad. They aren't perfect, but you love them. God chose them to be your parents. He knew exactly the kind of parents you needed. And, of course, it only makes sense that you obey them. You want to honor them. You want to make them proud of you.

So what did Jesus mean? As much as you want to please your parents, Jesus wants you to please *him* more. What *he* wants you to do matters more than anything else. He wants you to love him so much that your love for your folks seems like hatred by comparison. Get it? Jesus doesn't really want you to hate your parents. He was just making a comparison.

PRAYER Lord, how can I put you first in all I do and say? I know I will be tempted to do what I want, so I need you to help me obey you.

DAY 132

To all in Rome who are loved by God and called to be his holy people: Grace and peace to you from God our Father and from the Lord Jesus Christ.

–ROMANS 1:7

In this book of the Bible, Paul is writing to the church in Rome. So his greeting is specifically to the early church there. But as part of the Bible, this letter is timeless truth to all of Christ's followers. We might not live in Rome in the year AD 57, but we are all direct recipients of the wisdom of Paul and all of God's Word.

So, today, read the verse without "in Rome." Even cross out "all in Rome" and write in "you." Add your name if you want. "To you who are loved by God." Because you are called to be his holy child, grace and peace are yours. Those are pretty big gifts from some pretty big gift givers—your heavenly Father and the Lord Jesus Christ.

Paul doesn't say "Grace and peace are yours if you're lucky, if things are going your way, if people are being kind to you." He says because God is who he is and because Jesus did what he did, grace and peace are yours. Period. So today, remember that God loves you, you are his.

PRAYER

Thank you for your Word, Lord. I ask that you make grace and peace real for me as I learn about you and your Son.

DAY 133

Fill in the blanks. Which people from the Bible answer the puzzle questions below.

- This giant-killing shepherd said, "The Lord who rescued me from the paw of the lion and the paw of the bear will rescue me from the hand of this Philistine." 1 2 __ 3 __
- This physician followed Jesus and wrote the third gospel. 4 5 __ __
- This "helper" was created by God from Adam's rib. __ 6 7
- This writer of many New Testament letters changed his name from Saul. 8 __ __ __
- This man led the Israelites into the Promised Land after Moses died. 9 10 __ 11 __ __
- "I am the Lord's servant" said the one who gave birth in a stable. 12 __ 13 14
- The church's first martyr faced death saying, "I see heaven open and the Son of Man standing at the right hand of God." 15 16 __ __ __ __ 17

Now fill in the letters that go with the numbers. When you are finished, you will find out why we have peace, joy, and hope.

Titus 3:7—so that, _____ G B__ __ _____ F__ __
                    11 2 6 3 17   7 7 17 9 5 15 16 3 3 7 1

B__ _____ G__C__, we might B__C__ _____ _____
14 11 3 15 13 2 7   7 10 12 7 11 7 3 13 15

_____ G _____ _____ __ F _____ __ __ F .
11 2 6 3 17 16 11 7 11 10 8 7 10 7 16 7 13 17 2 4 4 3 7

144

DAY 134

What does it mean to be a servant? Who can you serve this week? Describe how.

_____

_____

_____

_____

_____

_____

DAY 135

But God demonstrates his own love for us in this:
While we were still sinners, Christ died for us.

−ROMANS 5:8

This is a true story. At the edge of a forest on a dusty dirt road, a truck backs up to a dumpster. There's a woman with a ladder in the back of the truck. When the truck comes to a stop, the woman carefully slides the ladder from the truck into the big metal dumpster, motions to the driver to pull away, and sits down as the truck edges away. The ladder, propped up in the dumpster, starts to shake. A fuzzy head pops up. Then two. Then three. One by one, sweet black bear cubs crawl up the ladder and climb onto the dumpster's edge. They jump to the ground. Once the bears are on the ground, a watchful mama bear appears from the forest and leads her cubs into the safety of the woods.

The rescue is heartwarming to watch. The woman saw the trapped bears and the helpless mama bear and went to rescue them. The bears did nothing but take the gift of the ladder.

In the same way, God arrived to rescue us. We can be trapped in the garbage of our own lives but we have been offered a way out—the cross. God sees us, loves us, and provides a rescue plan.

PRAYER I could never rescue myself. But you have rescued me and I can follow you for wisdom and love. Thank you, Father. Thank you, Jesus.

DAY 136

Do you not know that your bodies are temples of the Holy Spirit, who is in you, whom you have received from God? You are not your own; you were bought at a price. Therefore honor God with your bodies.

—1 CORINTHIANS 6:19-20

Physical exercise has spiritual perks. So does the amount of sleep you get. Even what you eat matters to God. Your body is his temple.

When Paul was writing to his friends in Corinth, he knew they were being pressured to do things with their bodies that were unhealthy. It broke his heart to realize how difficult it was for Christ-followers to resist peer pressure. But then it dawned on him that the real reason they should ask God's help to be strong, healthy, and pure was because their bodies weren't really theirs to begin with. Their bodies belonged to the Holy Spirit who lived in them.

How you take care of the body God has given you really does matter. A healthy body will allow you to live better and serve him longer. That means we can't just pig out or skip exercise. What we put into our bodies is an act of worship, and the way we use our bodies causes others to make conclusions about Jesus (good or bad).

PRAYER Lord, I want to be a beautiful temple for you to live. Give me the motivation to say yes to being healthy.

DAY 137

For he chose us in him before the creation of the world to be holy and blameless in his sight. In love he predestined us for adoption to sonship through Jesus Christ, in accordance with his pleasure and will.

-EPHESIANS 1:4-5

Don't shop. Adopt." That's the slogan that suggests people skip the pet store and find a puppy at a shelter. Dog shelters are full of animals that have been wandering lost in the street or were abandoned by their owners. Think of peeking in each cage, pointing to a puppy, and giving it hope with the phrase, "I want you. Be mine!" Wouldn't you be so excited to give a home to a dog that needed rescue? You could scrub her up, wrap her in love, make her safe.

God's delight comes in rescuing people. He goes to lost hearts and says, "I want you. Be mine." He loves to adopt and make us at home with him. He makes us clean, wraps us in love, makes us safe.

Where are you in your relationship with God? Are you still caged up or have you been rescued and adopted into a forever home? In love, he's waiting and saying, "I want you. Be mine."

PRAYER

Thank you for loving me, Lord, and looking out for me. I trust you to rescue me. Come into my heart.

DAY 138

For we are God's handiwork, created in Christ Jesus to do good works, which God prepared in advance for us to do.

—EPHESIANS 2:10

Can you remember the last time you created something—a picture, a sculpture, a dance, or a song? Maybe you made something for school, or created something with friends, or worked on something simply because you liked doing it? Did you show it proudly to your parents and grandparents or hang it on the fridge so others could enjoy it? After all, it was specially and lovingly labored over, and the results are a reflection of the unique artist.

Think of a creation you were especially fond of. That is how God thinks of you. You are a work of art, a prized masterpiece of a personal God.

Not only were you fashioned by God who loves you, you were saved by Jesus' sacrifice. You have been blessed by grace. Now it's time to share the blessing. That doesn't mean putting yourself in the spotlight for people to simply admire, nor does it involve bragging about your great gifts. It means sharing the blessing in good works. Your good works might be quiet and individual or big and ambitious. Look around. Once you open your eyes, God will show you the opportunity.

PRAYER Jesus, thank you for the blessing of salvation. Show me what to do now.

DAY 139

Children, obey your parents in the Lord, for this is right. "Honor your father and mother"—which is the first commandment with a promise—"so that it may go well with you and that you may enjoy long life on the earth."

–EPHESIANS 6:1-3

God notices you. He cares about what you do. He doesn't just look at the grown-ups and keep track of their lives. He cares about your choices too.

Here's a choice that comes up a lot: listening to your mom and dad.

It's easy to listen to Mom or Dad when you know the rules are good ones: "Don't run out in the road." "No computer for more than three hours at a time." "No eating brownies for breakfast." Most kids would agree with those rules—at least most of the time.

But it's a lot harder to listen to your parents when they say something that doesn't seem to make sense. They don't let you play with a friend or they make you eat lima beans. *What's the point?* you may think. So you might get mad, disobey, or do your own thing.

God's wish isn't that you listen only when it makes sense to you. He instructs you to obey your parents, period. God promises that as you honor them, "things will go well with you." That's a promise you can trust.

PRAYER Lord, help me to obey my mom and dad. Not just when it seems to makes sense to me, but all the time.

DAY 140

Name the pictures and discover how God sees you.

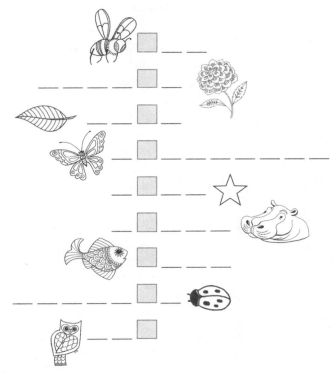

How _____ you are my darling! Oh how
_____.

–SONG OF SOLOMON 4:1A

DAY 141

God says he will never leave you. Write down all the places you'd like to visit and things you'd like to see. Pray about your plans and commit your dreams to God.

_____

_____

_____

_____

_____

TAKE DELIGHT IN THE LORD, & HE WILL GIVE YOU THE DESIRES OF YOUR HEART.

PSALM 37:4

DAY 142

It is true that some preach Christ out of envy and rivalry, but others out of goodwill . . . But what does it matter? The important thing is that in every way, whether from false motives or true, Christ is preached. And because of this I rejoice.

—PHILIPPIANS 1:15, 18

Think of the meanest kid you know. You would never expect him to read the Bible. Then one day you hear him telling his friends about the Golden Rule.

What? That kid takes the golden rule to the opposite extreme! Who does he think he is, telling other kids about acting nicely? The message came out of an ungodly mouth, so does that mean it's untrue? Not at all.

One of the confusing things for the Philippians was that certain people were spreading the good news of Jesus Christ for the wrong reasons. These people weren't trying to pass on the love of God. They were just trying to mess with the apostle Paul.

But this is the cool thing: Truth is truth no matter who says it. God is the author of truth. He may even use atheists to teach about morality and bullies to talk about kindness. After all, remember Balaam's donkey (Numbers 22).

PRAYER God, I don't understand how people who are anti-God could speak anything true or spread your good news. Please open my eyes to recognize your truth no matter who it comes from.

DAY 143

See to it that no one takes you captive through hollow and deceptive philosophy, which depends on human tradition and the elemental spiritual forces of this world rather than on Christ.

–COLOSSIANS 2:8

Paul probably felt like a juggler sometimes. As soon as he successfully launched one church, another often tumbled to the ground.

Take the church in Colossae. False teachers were insisting the Colossian Christians needed to worship angels and follow special rules and ceremonies in order to be saved. So Paul had to come to the rescue. Paul reminded the Colossians that following rules doesn't save us—only following Christ does. Maybe people don't tell you to worship angels today. But saying that religiously sticking to certain rules will save your soul still lives on. See if you can spot it in these sentences:

- "You weren't at church this week, so God is ticked off."
- "Good Christians only listen to worship music."
- "Wow, I can't believe you're wearing that shirt."

It's a good idea to follow rules. They guide and protect us. But instead of worshiping rules, God wants us to worship him. That's why Jesus died on the cross. When we ask him into our hearts, his sacrifice washes away our sins permanently. We are free!

PRAYER Jesus, thanks for becoming the final sacrifice for my sins. I don't want to cheapen that by making others' words more important than yours.

DAY 144

Therefore, as God's chosen people, holy and dearly loved, clothe yourselves with compassion, kindness, humility, gentleness, and patience.

–COLOSSIANS 3:12.

Imagine you see a person wearing a shirt that says: "God is love." And then she promptly cuts in front of you in line, curses to the waitress, and bumps a baby without apology. It would be a little shocking, right? Like she's advertising one thing, but delivering something else. Of course, no person can be a perfect representative of God, but we can do our best to bring honor to his name.

God has lavished grace, mercy, and compassion on us. If we truly realize we've received great gifts, it becomes easier to share it all with others. Having benefited from his unfailing love, we're equipped to pass the blessing on.

Sometimes it's easier to be defensive and harsh with uncaring, selfish people. But God has shown us kindness and patience. You are dearly loved and chosen by God himself. When the going gets hard, go to him first. Ask him to help you show patience and love even when it's the hard thing to do.

PRAYER Father, sometimes it's easy to be kind, gentle, and patient. And sometimes it's the hardest thing ever. But you have shown me love and mercy, and I want to pass on those blessings. Show me how.

DAY 145

You are all children of the light and children of the day. We do not belong to the night or to the darkness.

–1 THESSALONIANS 5:5

The flame from a single candle can light up an entire cathedral. The light of a single match can illuminate a whole cave. The light of a single star travels trillions of miles to shine in the dark sky. Darkness cannot stand up to light, even from the smallest source.

Jesus called himself and his disciples the Light of the World. Darkness cannot stand up to them. As we shine loving truth into our homes, schools, neighborhoods, and cities, no matter how small, it cuts through darkness.

Our entire ecosystem depends on Earth's great source of light—the sun. Animals, people, and plants couldn't survive without it. It is the perfect distance and temperature for Earth to survive.

God is the sun that our souls need to thrive and survive. We revolve around our Lord, who is our light and salvation.

PRAYER Thank you, God, that we don't have to hide in fear and darkness. Because I am your child, I walk in light. I want your warmth and light to shine in me and from me.

DAY 146

He must manage his own family well and see that his children obey him, and he must do so in a manner worthy of full respect.

−1 TIMOTHY 3:4

The apostle Paul provides a list of qualifications for those being considered for church leadership positions. One of the key qualifications was being a father of children who obey him. In other words, dads of disobedient daughters and sons would be left out. If they weren't successful leading their own children, how could they effectively help lead a congregation?

If you knew your behavior kept your father from becoming all God wanted him to be, would you try harder to do what you are told? Obeying your dad not only helps him; it helps you too!

Obeying your dad is a way of honoring your heavenly Father. When you show respect to your parents and do what they ask you to do, you are giving in to their authority. And that's what God wants us to do. It's his way of training us to do what he tells us to do in the Bible.

PRAYER Because I love my father, I don't want my poor behavior to stand in the way of what you have planned for him. Help me do what is right and what I'm told.

DAY 147

Use the key to crack the code and find out the secret message.

for you are a people
holy to the Lord your
God. The Lord your God
has chosen you out
of all the peoples, on
the face of the earth
to be his people, his
treasured possession.

Deuteronomy 7:6

♋	●	⌘		❖	◆	❀	♈	✝	❀
a	to	of		on	be	has	out	all	his
for	are	you		the	God	holy	Lord	face	chosen
your	earth	possession		peoples					
people	treasured								

DAY 148

God has created you for a purpose. What are some of your goals in life? What would you like to become?

_____
_____
_____
_____
_____
_____
_____

DAY 149

Listen, my dear brothers: Has not God chosen those who are poor in the eyes of the world to be rich in faith and to inherit the kingdom he promised those who love him?

–JAMES 2:5

If things of value were graded, earth and heaven would score things differently. Earth values popularity, fame, and fortune. It cherishes things you can acquire, achievements you can measure, and beauty you can see. On the other hand, God values qualities you can't see such as patience, self-control, and achievements you can't measure such as loving others.

The problem is we can get distracted by the things of earth. If we are focused on small and shallow things, we forget about the great things of God. So sometimes those who aren't distracted by their own fortune—the poor in the eyes of the world—can grow more in faith. The ones who aren't distracted by outer things can grow more on the inside.

So be encouraged to live above the distractions and value the things of heaven. That's right where your heavenly Father wants you.

PRAYER Jesus, I want my heart to be a place where faith can grow. Lead me in that direction. Remind me of the things you value.

DAY 150

See what great love the Father has lavished on us, that we should be called children of God.

−1 JOHN 3:1A

No dad is just like another. Some dads play board games, some play ball, some don't play at all. Some dads read, while others snuggle. Some serve cookies at tea parties, and some don't care for tea at all. There is a wide variety of great dads out there. There are also plenty of fathers whose brokenness makes it hard for them to do their best as a parent.

Here's the good news: our Father in heaven is perfect. He's always there. He covers us in love. He gives all kinds of gifts. He wants to keep company especially with you.

Maybe you have a great example of God in your dad— selfless, loving, close, and cozy. But maybe you don't. Still, you are loved by the perfect Father. He cares so much for you and wants to care for your heart. So smile and stand tall. You couldn't be more loved.

PRAYER

Jesus, I love you and am happy to call myself a child of God. Thank you for never abandoning me or getting tired of me and turning your back on me. Help me grow and trust in you.

DAY 151

I know your deeds; you have a reputation of being alive, but you are dead. Wake up! Strengthen what remains and is about to die, for I have found your deeds unfinished in the sight of my God.

–REVELATION 3:1-2

You want to become a concert pianist. You learn the basic notes, where to place your fingers, master "Chopsticks," and never play again. But you claim that you are now a concert pianist.

Um, that's not quite how it works.

Worthwhile things you choose to do take work and dedication. If you really want to be a concert pianist, you're going to practice hours and hours over a long period of time, memorizing music, and performing every chance you get. To become good enough for a professional concert, you might need to play for years, and then still keep practicing so you don't lose your skills.

Giving your life to God and calling yourself a Christian isn't a one-time deal either. You can confess your sin and ask Jesus Christ into your life, but that's not the end. He wants to grow your friendship with him. That takes dedication. And sometimes it might even feel like it takes practice. Are you ready to become a concert-worthy servant for God? He can't wait to make some beautiful music with you!

PRAYER God, there are many things I want to do with my life. Serving you needs to be first, but I need the dedication to do it. Please show me how great a champion I can be for you if I put in the time.

DAY 152

For the Lamb at the center of the throne will be their
shepherd; 'he will lead them to springs of living water.'
'And God will wipe away every tear from their eyes'.

−REVELATION 7:17

In the book of Revelation, we get glimpses of heaven and hints of eternity. The book is a puzzle with all its symbols and images, but it's also full of reassurance and encouragement for believers.

Jesus the Lamb is on the throne. And even in heaven, he does the Shepherd's work. He leads believers to springs of living water (the Holy Spirit). This is similar to what Psalm 23 says about our relationship with Jesus on Earth: "The Lord is my shepherd, I shall not be in want. He makes me lie down in green pastures, he leads me beside quiet waters, he restores my soul." In Revelation, he restores his flock in heaven. The lost have been found. The wandering are safe at the feet of the Shepherd. They thirst no more.

And even in eternity, the tenderness of the Father shines through. He personally will wipe each individual tear from the eyes of each precious one.

It's hard to picture heaven and how perfect it will be. But the same Father, Son, and Holy Spirit we walk with on Earth will be there, celebrating and rejoicing with us.

PRAYER

Oh Lord, I can't imagine no more sin and no more tears. But I'm grateful that you will be the same in heaven as you are now: my Good Shepherd.

DAY 153

Let us rejoice and be glad and give him glory! For the wedding of the Lamb has come, and his bride has made herself ready.

-REVELATION 19:7

Playing dress-up is guaranteed girly entertainment, and at the top of the list is often pretending to be a bride in a stunning wedding gown.

Guess what? If you have a personal relationship with Jesus, you have two weddings to look forward to. One is your marriage ceremony to your future husband here on Earth. And the other is a gigantic wedding in heaven to the Lord.

Of course, marrying God won't be like marrying a man. Instead, "the wedding of the Lamb" in Revelation 19:7 is when all who know Christ are finally united with him in heaven. Like a wedding reception, it's going to be one giant party.

Before that celebration kicks off, however, we have some work to do. Jesus wants our hearts and spirits to be beautiful for him. That means learning to become a mature Christian through prayer, Bible reading, time with other believers, and service to our community.

So when you follow God's commands you're not just obeying him. You're actually making yourself into a beautiful bride!

PRAYER Jesus, I'm excited to rejoice and be glad and give you glory. Help me remember that you're the most important person in my life.

SECTION 4

Be Encouraged

And I know whatever's gonna come my way

You're here with me and it's going

to be a good day

DAY 155

When you think of looking beautiful, what things come to mind? Write them here. When you think of being beautiful on the inside, what can you add to your list?

_____

_____

_____

_____

_____

_____

DAY 156

*Before he had finished praying, Rebekah came out
with her jar on her shoulder. She was the daughter of
Bethuel son of Milkah, who was the wife of Abraham's
brother Nahor.*

–GENESIS 24:15

Rebekah didn't make big decisions without her family. When faced with a decision, she called, "Hey, Mom!" Then she brought in her brother, her dad, and even the servants in their home. The family helped Rebekah decide to marry.

How important is your family? God created your family to give you a safe place to grow up. Whether you have brothers or sisters or one parent or grandparents, your family will be part of your life forever. Sure, you'll argue and get upset with each other. But overall, your family is there to help you—no matter what.

Can you do the same for your family? Does your younger sibling need help with homework? When your mom is sick, can you help with extra chores? How loud can you cheer at your cousin's track meet? Stand up for your family. Thank them for being there for you. Be there for them. And when a big decision comes, you'll know whom to call.

PRAYER

God, please show me how to be helpful and supportive of my family, even when I'm not happy with them.

DAY 157

Then the angel of God, who had been traveling in front of Israel's army, withdrew and went behind them. The pillar of cloud also moved from in front and stood behind them, coming between the armies of Egypt and Israel.

−EXODUS 14:19-20

What comes to mind when you think about angels? Wings? White robes? Glowing beings floating and gliding about? The Israelites got to see angels, but the angels weren't like the pictures you see in books or movies. The angels who protected the people leaving Egypt showed up in the form of massive pillars of fire and clouds. In truth, angels come in several forms, depending on their mission from God. Angels are God's messengers and watchers. They have particular jobs on Earth and in heaven.

While humans don't get to see angels often, sometimes they appear in person. Angels may also appear in dreams. Most of the time, you can't see what's going on in the heavenly world, but the angels carry out God's work. They always praise God, and often, they protect people. The angel Michael is known as the protector of the Israelites (or Jews). Gabriel is the angel who announced the birth of Jesus Christ. God even sends people as "angels" to help someone in need.

PRAYER Lord, thank you for the angels who work for you and help protect my family and me.

DAY 158

And Joshua set up at Gilgal the twelve stones they had taken out of the Jordan. He said to the Israelites, "In the future when your descendants ask their parents, 'What do these stones mean?' tell them, 'Israel crossed the Jordan on dry ground.'"

–JOSHUA 4:20-22

Do you know anyone who has a rock collection? Collecting rocks isn't as popular today as it once was but you might know some girls who collect stuffed animals, hair accessories, or charms.

Joshua's rock collection was different. The stones he collected and piled up were from a river that dried up for one special day. That was the amazing day the Lord pushed back the waters of the Jordan River so the Israelites could walk across to the Promised Land. That miracle was a day worth celebrating in Israel's history. Joshua didn't want the people to forget what God had done for them. So he piled up the rocks to remind them. Then their children and grandchildren could ask about the rocks and be told what God had done.

Ask your grandparents to tell you stories about God in their lives. Think on the times God has blessed you or your family. Maybe even start your own rock pile to symbolize his goodness.

PRAYER Lord, I want to collect stories of the way you answer prayer. Please don't let me forget the many ways you come through for us.

DAY 159

They married Moabite women, one named Orpah and the other Ruth. After they had lived there about ten years, both Mahlon and Kilion also died, and Naomi was left without her two sons and her husband.

−RUTH 1:4-5

Naomi had reason to be sad. Her husband and two sons died. Wow! Can you imagine anything worse than that? The people she loved the most were gone. Besides being sad, Naomi was very lonely.

Death is part of our lives. There is no way to avoid it. You are old enough to understand that loss leaves us with tears and aches in our hearts. Jesus knows exactly how it feels too. He cried when people he loved here on earth died. But he also knew that the Father has a bigger plan that includes life after death. And that knowledge takes away some of the sting.

Since the beginning of sin, God hated how death affected us. That's one of the reasons Jesus died on the cross and rose from the grave. He wanted to show death who was boss. Because of what Jesus did, death was defeated. Like everyone, those who love Jesus will eventually close their eyes in death, but their eyes will open in heaven.

PRAYER Lord, death bothers me. I'm glad it bothered you enough to do something about it, but it still makes me sad.

DAY 160

*Because the LORD had closed Hannah's womb, her
rival kept provoking her in order to irritate her. This
went on year after year. Whenever Hannah went up to
the house of the LORD, her rival provoked her till she
wept and would not eat.*

–1 SAMUEL 1:6-7

Peninah was a mean girl. We don't know why, but she bullied,
insulted, and picked on Hannah. For years, Peninah made
fun of Hannah, sometimes until Hannah would cry and leave the
dinner table. And they were part of the same family.

Sometimes girls can be really mean. They pick on each other,
leave each other out, and laugh at each other. You might not realize when you hurt someone else with what you say. Perhaps you
like to joke around and think your friends and family understand
your sense of humor. But no matter what, be careful with your
words. If you have to bury your face in a pillow and scream, that's
better than saying something mean. How would you feel if someone picked on you until you cried? Even if that person was joking,
getting your feelings hurt is never fun. Instead, stay away from
the mean girls and be a girl who uses her words for praise.

PRAYER
Lord, I know I've hurt others with my words before.
Please forgive me for being mean.

DAY 161

Search up, down, and sideways to find the words in the verse below. (Repeating words will be found once.)

"Though the mountains be shaken and the hills be removed, yet my unfailing love for you will not be shaken nor my covenant of peace be removed," says the LORD, who has compassion on you.

–ISAIAH 54:10

```
D E J N U B T B G B T O I L J R K H A G
G P C Y O O I N V L H Q R T C H N A V Q
Z M I A N I I T Y U O X V O T S R T F A
T E E Y E L S Y X L U Y R U F N T P F V
R F X M I P N S J K G H V T Q I H S F L
B B L A K Q C I A B H A L K A A E B Y H
G R F L X J V R G P G S O B U T L N H C
O N F E S H Q E E T M D N Y H N Y S M O
U Z P K G N L H J N W O U U N U K A J Y
T M T U S A G O A P S H C L B O X T R H
L L V O N A G X R Y X G O H V M P P E T
D E I Y Y C V W B D O K U U N K A I J U
L L W W T N A E N O Y S A X T U J C O O
S K R D J N M V M I W B R A I S L L I H
F F E P C Y G O X V X X N E H L L R C P
D W F I S U T L C O D D D A M L Y L N C
V O E O C O V E N A N T K L I O V Z K K
Q H S V N N Q Q O G F E C W C F V T E V
A A V S A Y S N O R N P Y G Y X B E A R
W S D G W C G O B I L S R O O Y L Z D I
```

AND	HILLS	NOT	THE	YET
COMPASSION	LORD	PEACE	THOUGH	YOU
COVENANT	LOVE	REMOVED	UNFAILING	
FOR	MOUNTAINS	SAYS	WHO	
HAS	NOR	SHAKEN	WILL	

DAY 162

Write down some of the nicest things others have said to you or done for you.

_____
_____
_____
_____
_____
_____

DAY 163

Then King David went in and sat before the Lord, and he said: "Who am I, Lord God, and what is my family, that you have brought me this far?"

−1 CHRONICLES 17:16

It can be easy to forget how good we have it: a warm bed, food on the table, a shower, family, and friends. So many people don't have the simple things we enjoy every day. To live under a roof is a huge gift, but when is the last time we were thankful for the roof that protects us from wind, rain, and snow?

Make a habit of thanking God for all the things he has given to you: clothes, a school, friends, peanut butter and jelly sandwiches, running water . . . Consider all the ways he has provided, and thank him for the way he has taken care of you.

Once your eyes are open to blessings, it becomes easier to see them.

Even if you are facing hard things, such as waiting for a family to adopt you, hoping your mom gets better from a long sickness, or praying for money to pay for a new car, look for something to be grateful for. It might be small, like the chirping of a bird, or big, like God who is seeing you through. He will protect you and continue to give you good things along the way.

PRAYER

Lord, thank you for the good things you have given me. I know I sometimes take them for granted or have a hard time seeing what's good. Open my eyes.

DAY 164

And you, my son Solomon, acknowledge the God of your father, and serve him with wholehearted devotion and with a willing mind, for the LORD searches every heart and understands every desire and every thought.

−1 CHRONICLES 28:9

A lot of dads teach their children how to ride a bike and kick a soccer ball. Some show their children how to catch fish and clean them. Dads who ski may teach their children how to approach a downhill slope.

But the most important thing a father can teach his child is what King David taught his son Solomon: to love and obey God. The king could have given the prince all kinds of things, but he knew his son's relationship with the Lord was the key to everything else.

Notice the words David used. Wholehearted devotion. Willing mind. This dad knew that it takes all you have to serve the Lord. You can't just play around with being a God follower. You have to practice your faith just like you practice riding a bike. The fact that you are reading this today means you're already making progress and taking some fatherly advice.

PRAYER

Lord, I'm grateful for the gift of fathers. And I'm grateful for you. Strengthen my relationship with you.

DAY 165

For forty years you sustained them in the wilderness; they lacked nothing, their clothes did not wear out nor did their feet become swollen.

—NEHEMIAH 9:21

A day-long hike up a mountain trail can do you in. An uphill climb leaves you thirsty, hungry, and tired. Every two or three miles you have to "take five." And when you stop to rest, you're grateful there's some trail mix along with that cold water in your bottle. By the end of the day, your feet are aching and your legs feel like lead.

So can you imagine going on a forty-year hike? Our spiritual ancestors did that after escaping slavery! Although the distance to their destination was in reality only a two-week walk, God led them the long way through the wilderness to the Promised Land. He'd successfully gotten them out of Egypt, but the Lord realized it would take some time to get "Egypt" out of them.

The Lord wanted to wean his people from self-destructive attitudes and teach them to trust him. To win them over, he provided food, shelter, clothing, and comfort. Just imagine: There was always enough to eat, and their gear never wore out.

As we hike through the ups and downs of life, the Lord promises to provide for our needs too. All we need to do is follow his lead, even if it might be the long way.

PRAYER Lord, I'm grateful for the many ways you provide for my needs. Thanks for a place to sleep, food to eat, and clothes to wear. Forgive me when I complain about not having more.

DAY 166

Your own conduct and actions have brought this on you. This is your punishment. How bitter it is! How it pierces to the heart!" Oh, my anguish, my anguish! I writhe in pain. Oh, the agony of my heart.

–JEREMIAH 4:18-19

It is no fun when your parents ground you or take away your allowance. Don't you wish they would just let you do whatever you want? Would you believe that if they allowed you to do whatever you wanted, they wouldn't be showing you love? Wait a minute! Discipline and love go together?

Think about it this way: Suppose your mom never told you NOT to stick your fingers in the electrical outlets, and then when you did, she just shrugged her shoulders and said, "Too bad." You would be upset that she didn't stop you from frying your fingers (and maybe the ends of your hair!).

You might not like hearing "No" and "Don't do that" and "I said stop." But your parents say those things to protect you.

God is the same with his children. He shows us how to live under his guidance. He cautions us not to leave his protection. If he has to, he warns more than once—like he did with Israel.

Discipline is a reminder of real love. If you pay attention to your parents' and God's words, then you show them you love them enough to obey. That's a love-love situation.

PRAYER Lord, discipline is no fun at all. And I don't always understand your instructions or my parents'. Please let me see how you are all looking out for me with love.

DAY 167

*"For I know the plans I have for you," declares the
LORD, "plans to prosper you and not to harm you, plans
to give you hope and a future."*

−JEREMIAH 29:11

What's the weather like where you live? Do you get all four seasons? Do you have mostly sun or do you get dumped on with snow? Do you have colorful autumns or ice storms, torrential rain or tornadoes? The weather we all have in common is the weather that changes all the time.

Life is like the weather. It never stays the same. Sometimes it's smooth sailing: you're rocking it at school; you're getting along with your friends; you got the lead part in a play. And sometimes a storm blows in: a sickness slows you down; your family decides to move; someone hurts your feelings. When something hard happens, it feels like you're standing in the cold rain.

God says there is promise even in the storms of life. Because the One who hangs rainbows in dark skies gives you hope through all the weather of life. The God in the storm is the God of your future, offering you hope and purpose and big plans. No matter what you face, focus on his light.

PRAYER Lord, thank you for letting me know you are with me through sunshine and rain. I will look for your promises like rainbows in the sky.

DAY 168

Starting at the arrow, go around the circle to the right. Write every other letter in the spaces provided to find out what encouragement 1 Peter 5:7 offers.

_____ ____ _____ _____ __

____ _____ __ _____ ____

____.

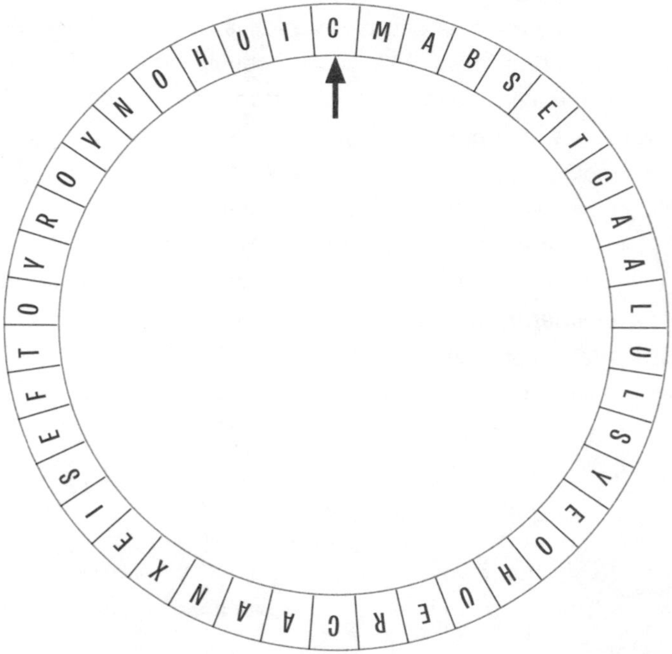

DAY 169

Write about one of the biggest changes you have ever faced in life. Who helped you get through it? How?

_____

_____

_____

_____

_____

_____

DAY 170

*Because of the L****ORD****'s great love we are not consumed,*
for his compassions never fail. They are new every
morning; great is your faithfulness.

–LAMENTATIONS 3:22-23

When you get in a car, what is the first thing you do after shutting the door? Put on your seatbelt, of course! Then when the road gets bumpy, or swervy, you are solid. Sure, you feel the bumps, but you don't hit your head on the roof. You lean at the turns, but you don't slam to the other side.

Life can be a bumpy ride. Your day can take a sudden wrong turn and things at home or school or with your friends can change in an instant. So it's important to remember to put on your seatbelt every day. That is, focus on God's lasting love. Remind yourself that his faithfulness is great and his compassion toward you never fails. Remember that God is in the driver's seat. Then during a rough day, you will notice *him* in the bumps and not get lost among the potholes of life.

PRAYER

Okay, God, I'm putting on my seatbelt. I'm giving you the steering wheel. Because I trust you and know how much you love me, I'm ready for the road ahead.

DAY 171

Therefore prophesy and say to them: 'This is what the Sovereign Lord says: My people, I am going to open your graves and bring you up from them; I will bring you back to the land of Israel.

—EZEKIEL 37:12

Finally! Ezekiel gets to bring some good news. But first he has to go through what seems like a haunted Halloween path—a valley of dry bones. This guy isn't scared, though. He's seen so many crazy and amazing things that a valley of bones that come to life doesn't faze him one bit.

Though Ezekiel's story reads like a scary dream, it isn't. God's message is about life: Nothing is impossible for him. His people had become so evil they were destroyed and left for dead. Now it was time for him to do his work of redemption.

Redemption turns something that has no value or use into a treasure. God can bring life from death. He can turn a desert into a lush valley. And if he wants, he can turn a valley of bones into new living creations.

Even when it seems like sin has won and taken every last bit of life out of someone, God says, "Not so fast. I have the last say!"

PRAYER God, I can't imagine watching a valley of bones come to life. You can do anything, and I want my faith to be strong enough to believe that you can use anything and anyone.

DAY 172

Let us acknowledge the Lᴏʀᴅ; let us press on to acknowledge him. As surely as the sun rises, he will appear; he will come to us like the winter rains, like the spring rains that water the earth.

–HOSEA 6:3-4

You could travel anywhere in the world and the sun would still rise every day. In any country, near or far, you could ask, "Will the sun rise tomorrow?" And the answer would be, "Yes."

Just like the sun, the moon will always rise, the ocean will always shift tides, and the seasons will change. They are set in creation to happen at a certain time. They will never change. Guess where that comes from? God's nature. He is unchanging and consistent. He will always be a loving, all-powerful, all-knowing God. He will always hear prayers. He will always forgive a repentant heart.

Nature itself is a witness that God exists. Without a consistent unchanging God in charge of the universe, nature would be chaotic and unpredictable. Pray that God will send his messengers around the world to tell others of the One who created the things they can count on.

PRAYER | Lord, nature shows me so much about who you are. Just like I can expect the sun to rise and set every day, I can expect you to love me and hear my prayers. Thank you.

DAY 173

My thoughts trouble me and I am distraught because
of what my enemy is saying, because of the threats of
the wicked; for they bring down suffering on me and
assail me in their anger.

–PSALM 55:2A-3

Can you remember when someone said something mean or hurtful about you? Those comments are usually pretty hard to forget. King David didn't like it either. It seems strange that people would dare attack the king. What were they thinking?

When other people attack you, use a David technique to help you deal with it: Put it on paper. If like King David, you like to write, then use words to convey what has happened and how you feel. You could write a letter, poem, or a song. If you like painting or drawing, create a picture. Putting it on paper will help you get it out of your heart and head. Then ask God to turn the situation into something good. Like King David, tell God how you feel, how it hurts, how unfair things seem. Remember that you aren't alone, that a powerful and present God has your back. He will help you rise above the insult and move on.

PRAYER God, it hurts when others say mean things about me. Sometimes I just want to get back at them. Help me to care more about what you say than what others say.

185

DAY 174

Satisfy us in the morning with your faithful love so that we may shout with joy and be glad all our days.

–PSALM 90:14

Have you ever noticed that when you're hungry, that's all you can think about? Even if you're trying to listen to someone, a growling stomach seems louder than anything else in the room. An empty stomach won't be ignored until you fill it.

It can be the same when you're spiritually empty. You don't see or hear things clearly until you fill up with God. Remind yourself who God is and what his character is all about. Remind yourself that he's faithful, he listens and loves you. When you fill up on that good news, you can face your day with a clearer perspective, peace, and gladness.

Filling up on God is a regular, daily process, just like we need to fill up on nutrients every day. It's not like you can just eat a whole bunch one week and skip all your meals the next, right? So take some time every day to touch base with God—pray and read his Word. Fill up.

PRAYER

I come to you now, Lord. Fill me up with your faithful love. I know it takes time. So I want to commit to coming to you constantly, looking for spiritual nutrition.

DAY 175

Which places from the Bible answer the puzzle questions below.

- Our Savior was born in this little town of
  _ _ _ 1 _ 2 _ _ _ _
- Joshua fought the battle at _ _ _ 3 _ _ 4 where the walls came tumbling down
- Israel's capital of city _ _ 5 _ _ _ _ _ 6 fell
- The Israelites were slaves in _ _ _ _ 7
- Jesus walked on water on the Sea of _ 8 _ _ 9 _ _
- God told Jonah to go to _ _ _ _ 10 _ _
- Saul (later Paul) heard the voice of Jesus on the road to 11 _ _ _ _ 12 _ _

Now fill in the letters that go with the numbers. When you are finished, you will find out why with Jesus, we can take heart.

I have told you these things, so that in me you may have peace. In this world you will have trouble. But take heart!

___ ___ ___ ___ ___ ___ ___ ___ ___ ___ ___ ___ ___
3   1 8 10 2   4 10 2 5 12 4- 6   2

___ ___ ___ ___(w) ___ ___ ___ ___ .
7   1   2   4   5   9 11

−JOHN 16:33

187

DAY 176

Write a poem about God's love on the lines below.

_____

_____

_____

_____

_____

_____

DAY 177

Not to us, Lord, not to us but to your name be the glory, because of your love and faithfulness.

–PSALM 115:1

Have you noticed football players praising God in the end zone lately? As teams fight their way yard after yard, down after down, someone is bound to score a goal. Then right after the goal, it's becoming more and more common to see the player point to the sky, make the sign of the cross, or get down on one knee and bow his head.

Some guys may do that to show off—that they think they are awesome—but many do it to give God the glory. In a very public way, players want to acknowledge that God is the one who made them good at football, the one who gave them the chance to play. They believe in God and this is another way to praise his name.

Why not raise your hands toward heaven after getting an A on a test or winning at a gymnastics meet? Well, maybe that's a bit much, but how can you show praise to God for your accomplishments?

PRAYER You are worthy of my praise, God. Every time I accomplish something, it's all because of how you made me.

DAY 178

My comfort in my suffering is this: Your promise preserves my life.

-PSALM 119:50

Have you ever felt like things in your life were turning upside down or inside out? Maybe you had to face something completely unfamiliar: a new school, a new neighborhood, a new step-sibling. Maybe you had to learn something painfully new: walking on crutches, writing with a cast on your arm, daily treatments for asthma. Life can be full of growing pains.

When things change a lot on the outside or there is turmoil on the inside, it can feel like you're in the middle of a storm. When everything is unpredictable, God should be your oasis from the crazy. When nothing feels stable and everything feels new, God is dependable. His love is rock solid. His presence is unwavering. His comfort wraps around you like a super soft blanket.

Take it from David who wrote Psalm 119. He knew turmoil in his life. His house was sometimes chaotic. Yet in all his messy moments, his lasting, reliable place to run to was the tender, loving heart of God.

PRAYER Lord, I know you see my messiness and angst. My reassurance is that I can cry out to you and you hear me. Give me wisdom and comfort, Lord.

DAY 179

Children are a heritage from the LORD, offspring a reward from him.

—PSALM 127:3

A mom and dad rush to the hospital to have a baby. A day later, they leave with the baby held high in the sky and a big blue ribbon pinned to its blanket. A crowd cheers as they exit the hospital doors. It feels like a big awards ceremony.

Okay, so that's not usually what happens when a new baby arrives. And when guests come for dinner, your parents don't dress you up and place you on a podium and say, "Look at our prize daughter." But they could. Parents have every right to be proud of you. Know why?

Children are a reward from God. Whether you are a biological or adopted child, your parents "won" a huge blessing when you came into their lives.

PRAYER

God, thanks for giving me to my parents. I want to act like the reward you say I am. Will you help me do that?

DAY 180

The LORD is gracious and compassionate, slow to anger and rich in love.

–PSALM 145:8

It doesn't take much to make an elephant angry. If someone (even another elephant) is threatening its herd, an elephant can run twenty-five miles an hour to flatten the offender. And their anger doesn't leave quickly. The longest recorded elephant-versus-elephant fight was ten hours, fifty-six minutes.

Elephants aren't exactly cuddly creatures. But pachyderm anger is necessary. God gave elephants ferocious, aggressive instincts to physically protect themselves and their families.

Humans, however, are different. Though anger can be positive (remember Jesus clearing out the temple?), people often take it too far. Sometimes we feel like we need to tiptoe around friends, siblings, parents, or coaches who seem constantly angry. Or maybe we are that angry.

Sometimes God can be an angry God. But as the ultimate heavenly Father, he doesn't freak out over every mistake. Instead, he shows compassion and grace. (If you were raised in an angry, unforgiving household, it's easy to think that God is like that all the time. But he's not!) He's not eager to smash you under his giant foot. Instead, he's gently waiting for your return to his loving arms.

PRAYER God, it's hard to believe you're not angry when I blow it. Will you rewire my heart so I'll realize that you want to help me, not flatten me?

DAY 181

Whoever heeds discipline shows the way to life, but whoever ignores correction leads others astray.

–PROVERBS 10:17

What's the punishment in your house for not finishing your chores or for yelling at your parents? Time out, being grounded, or missing out on a sleepover? No one likes to get in trouble. The punishment, though, makes you think twice before you disobey again. Here's a surprise: Kids aren't the only ones who get disciplined. Adults face it too, but they don't lose their allowance or go to time out. Ask your mom to tell you about a time she got in trouble as a grown-up. You'll be surprised. Then ask your mom what she learned from it.

Everyone would agree that discipline is not fun. Being corrected by those in authority—parents, teachers, pastors—is part of learning. Think about it. If your mom didn't scold you for leaving a curling iron on, then some day you might accidentally start a fire in the bathroom. Correction can make you smarter—if you pay attention. While it's not fun to be disciplined, learn from it so you don't make the same mistake again. Just ask your mom.

PRAYER God, it's no fun getting in trouble at home or school. Sometimes I think my parents just want to spoil my fun. Let me see how I can learn from my mistakes.

DAY 182

Use the key to crack the code and find out the secret message.

```
_ _ _ _ _ _ _ _ _ _ _ _ _ _ _ _ _ _
      7       1   2   1       2   3       1
_ _ _ _ _ _ _ _ _ _ _ _ _ _ _ _ ! _ _
  3   4     1       10        8        4
_ _ _ _ _ _ _ _ _ _ _ _ _ _ _ _
  5       2       3     5   6       1
_ _ _ _ _ _ _ _ _ _ _ _
  6   7     4       2   10    9
_ _ _ _ _ _ _ _ _ _ _ _ _
  3       10      1           2
_ _ _ _ _ _ _ _ _ _ _ _ _ _ _ ,
  3   10      8       4     1   5
_ _ _ _ _ _ _ _ _ _ _ _ _ _ _
  3     2   7       5           6
_ _ _ _ _ _ _ _ , _ _ _ _
  8     6     4         5   8
_ _ . _ _ _ _ _ _ _ _ _
  7     8       5       9     9
_ _ _ _ _ _ _ _ ... 1 Peter 1:3-4
  4   3     9   10
```

1	2	3	4	5
be	to	of	in	he
the	God	and	our	his
Lord	into	hope	from	dead
Given	great	mercy	birth	spoil
Father	resurrection	heaven	perish	inheritance

6	7	8	9	10
us	an	or	is	a
has	new	can	for	you
that	fade	this	kept	Jesus
never	praise	Christ	living	through

DAY 183

What advice would you give your mom or dad if you could?

_____

_____

_____

_____

_____

_____

DAY 184

Hopes placed in mortals die with them; all the promise of their power comes to nothing.

-PROVERBS 11:7

The world is filled with powerful people. Kings, queens, presidents, prime ministers, governors, and mayors to name a few.

A person with power is able to get other people to do things. So that means you personally know some people who have power. The principal of your school. The pastor of your church. Your parents. Even the popular kids have power to sway other kids. It is natural to look up to people who have more power than you do. Often they become like heroes. They have control over things you don't, so it feels easy to trust them. Having them around makes us feel safe.

But even powerful people can't do everything. And powerful people don't live forever. Nobody does. No wonder King Solomon warns us not to get too starry-eyed with people. Sure, it's okay to have heroes. You can learn a lot from grownups who have special abilities and influence. But don't worship them. Don't expect them to be perfect. They can't be. Human beings, even the most powerful ones, can let you down. They are not God.

PRAYER Lord, sometimes it's hard to trust you because I can't see you. It's easier to admire others more than you sometime. But you are the only one who will never let me down.

DAY 185

Hope deferred makes the heart sick, but a longing fulfilled is a tree of life.

–PROVERBS 13:12

What are your dreams? Do you want to sing your heart out? Dance on Broadway? Write the next great novel? Now think about the simple day-to-day things. Maybe you want to do well in school, have a best friend you can count on, and get along with your siblings. When something we hope for doesn't happen, it can be tough.

God understands that it's frustrating when you don't accomplish exactly what you want. He won't come down and give you a big ol' bear hug, but God might use someone or something to cheer you up. He might create a blazing sunset or have your mom make your favorite cookies.

God cares about your hopes and dreams, but not everything you wish for is from him. If you keep your heart set on something that is out of your reach and God has not confirmed that he is part of it, your heart can become quite sad. Instead, give your hopes over to God. Ask him to turn them into reality or change your focus.

PRAYER

Lord, you know my hopes and dreams. You know the ones I've had to put off and you understand how much that hurts. Thank you for caring about me.

DAY 186

God is our refuge and strength, an ever-present help in trouble.

–PSALM 46:1

Because people are often lost, stuck, and hurt, there are a lot of offers out there for support and comfort. Buy this lucky charm! This book has all the answers! Use this crystal! The obvious problem is that none of those things have any power. They were dreamed up, carved out, and mass produced. You, however, have a direct line to the Creator himself. The One who sees all, knows all, has authority over all is with you! His help is true and complete.

God not only has power to help, but he wants to help. Nothing delights him more than when his child comes to him with her open heart. He comforts the hopeless, gives wisdom to the troubled, and leads the way for the lost. There is nothing he can't make clean. Nothing is too sad that he can't bring joy. Nothing is too big that he can't defeat.

Don't put your faith in counterfeits when the One who has seen it all and knows it all is waiting for you.

PRAYER Thank you, Father, for always, being with me. In joy and trouble, you are faithful. I am grateful.

DAY 187

The simple believe anything, but the prudent give thought to their steps.

−PROVERBS 14:15

You know the girl who believes anything. You could tell her, "McDonald's is giving out free meals if you can stand on your head in front of the counter for ten minutes." Off she'd go to the closest Mickey D's while you are standing there rolling your eyes.

Joking around is one thing (as long as no one gets hurt), but Proverbs cautions about believing everything you hear. Sometimes it's easy to figure out what's real and what's a scam. Other times, you may be tricked by a gimmick or an opportunity that sounds too good to be true. (It probably is!)

What's the big deal? Well, being gullible about silly little things can lead to believing lies about yourself, God, and others. That's why wisdom is important. Wisdom helps you discern—to know what's real and what's true. Wisdom develops when you pay attention in school, obey your parents, and learn the Bible. Then no one will be able to pull a fast one on you.

PRAYER

Lord, I want to learn what's real and true. Please grow me in your wisdom.

DAY 188

You will keep in perfect peace those whose minds are steadfast, because they trust in you.

−ISAIAH 26:3

A steadfast mind is one that is committed and dedicated, in particular to God. It focuses above earth-bound circumstances because it knows that God sits above worldly things, that his ways are higher, and that he is in control. When we can adopt a trusting heart and lay our burdens at his feet with confidence, then perfect peace follows.

Peter learned this lesson in a dramatic way—while walking *on* water. As Jesus walked on the sea, he looked at Peter in the boat and said, "Come." Peter immediately swung his legs over the side and hopped out onto the water. His eyes fixed on Jesus, he took a few steps. But then he looked down. As the waves rolled, he lost focus and started to sink.

If you focus on your circumstances, you'll sink into worry. Focus on Jesus to rise above in peace. You don't have to be super spiritual to pull it off. Simply ask Jesus to bring you along. He loves a willing heart. Remember: Eyes up! Head up! Mind on him! Your heart will naturally follow.

PRAYER Lord, perfect peace sounds great, but I can't do it by myself. Remind me to focus on you and trust.

DAY 189

Write the words of the verse in the crossword puzzle. (Hint: Start with the longest word.)

I call on the LORD in my distress, and he answers me.

-PSALM 120:1

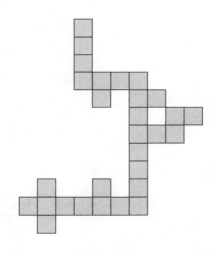

DAY 190

Today I'm going to trust God with these three things:

_____

_____

_____

_____

_____

HE
CARES FOR
THOSE
WHO
TRUST
IN HIM.
NAHUM 1:7

DAY 191

Then will the eyes of the blind be opened and the ears of the deaf unstopped. Then will the lame leap like a deer, and the mute tongue shout for joy.

–ISAIAH 35:5-6

Medical technology has created glasses and hearing aids and medicines to cure diseases. But many people are still blind, deaf, and sick. Around the world, approximately three hundred million people—more or less the population of the United States—are visually impaired or blind.

Long before we had doctors who could figure out how to do cornea replacements and laser vision correction, Jesus came to earth with healing power. The prophet Isaiah knew Jesus' coming would amaze people. And it did. By just a touch of his hand or a word from his mouth Jesus could open blind eyes, unstop deaf ears, and cure lifetime illnesses. He had no special equipment or surgical team to help him. He had the miraculous power of God.

One day he will heal all diseases and cure every ailment. Sickness and broken bodies will no longer be a problem for anyone. What a joyous and happy day that will be! People who lived in Israel during Jesus' time already got to see those miracles. One day everyone else will see them.

PRAYER Jesus, you did some awesome miracles on earth. I hope to see one someday! But I praise and thank you for the people you have blessed with skills to develop healing technology.

DAY 192

Jesus went throughout Galilee, teaching in their synagogues, proclaiming the good news of the kingdom, and healing every disease and sickness among the people.

–MATTHEW 4:23

You know how you feel sad some days or how bad you feel when you have to stay home sick? Maybe you have a family member who has cancer or a disability and can't play at recess or gym class.

When Jesus, God's Son, came to Earth, many people were sick and disabled. They didn't have any way to rush to an emergency room or a doctor's office. Often those who were sick had to sit out in the streets and beg for food and clothing. This made Jesus very sad. So when it was time to tell people about God's love and salvation, Jesus started healing people. He wanted them to see how amazing God's power is. Disfigured arms and legs, terrible sicknesses, blindness, and deafness were no match for God's power. He didn't need medicine to heal them. He just touched people with his hands or spoke a word and they were healed.

Did you know God still heals people today? He cares about sad hearts, broken bones, cancer, and even sinple headaches. Pray for your family when they are sick or hurt. Ask God to send his healing power like he did when his Son was on Earth.

PRAYER Lord, will you let me see your healing power? When I'm sick or a friend is hurt, I will ask you for healing.

DAY 193

"Look at the birds of the air, they do not sow or reap or store away in barns, and yet your heavenly Father feeds them. Are you not much more valuable than they? Can any one of you by worrying add a single hour to your life?"

—MATTHEW 6:26-27

The beginning of the Old Testament describes God's creation of the world. From the sun to the moon, from the land to the water, from the animals in the meadow to the animals in the sea, he created it all. And it was all good. Then on the sixth day, God created man. Man wasn't just good. He said: "It's very good!" From the beginning, people captured the heart of the Creator.

The beginning of the New Testament reminds us how much God cares for people. He takes care of creation, down to the smallest sparrow. Isn't he then going to take care of his children, his beloved who he called "very good"?

Have you ever heard the song, "He's got the whole world in his hands"? That's what this verse above is saying. He's got the sun and the moon . . . he's got the little busy bird . . . and he's got the one who is even more valuable—YOU!

PRAYER

Lord, instead of worrying, I'm going to talk to you. Thank you for always listening. And thank you for loving me so much.

DAY 194

Jesus answered them, "Destroy this temple, and I will raise it again in three days." They replied, "It has taken forty-six years to build this temple, and you are going to raise it in three days?"

—JOHN 2:19–20

Jesus liked to teach by speaking in riddles or metaphors. The people back then were sometimes confused by Jesus' metaphors and often came to the wrong conclusion. Or they just ignored him because they didn't really want to understand.

When you don't understand something in the Bible, don't dismiss it. Listening with your ears is one thing. Listening with your heart is even more important. If you pray for your heart to receive it, God will help.

Sometimes you'll figure out something on your own. Sometimes you'll want to hear an adult write or talk about it. And sometimes you'll get it as you grow and learn more about God's character.

It's important to learn God's words and study them. God will help you understand it at the right time.

PRAYER

Jesus, forgive me when I ignore your word because I didn't get it. I want to understand and hunt for what you mean to teach me.

DAY 195

The royal official said, "Sir, come down before my child dies."
"Go," Jesus replied, "your son will live."
The man took Jesus at his word and departed. While he was still on the way, his servants met him with the news that his boy was living.

–JOHN 4:49–51

The royal official had servants, position, status, and money. But the most important thing he had was faith. He knew none of his possessions or people could save a life. So he left his stuff behind. He had go find the one he knew could save his son's life.

When he heard Jesus's words, he had hope and took Jesus at his word. That is, the official believed everything Jesus said. He believed Jesus was who he said he was. And he believed that Jesus knew his son would not die. Indeed the boy was healed at the exact time that Jesus said to him, "Your son will live." Because of God's faithfulness and the attention of the Savior, the official and his whole household believed. Their faith grew, and they followed the Lord.

The man's faith in God's power took him away from all this life had to offer, and he found the one who saves. Take your faith and go find the one who offers encouragement, wisdom, peace, and life.

PRAYER

Lord, I'm encouraged by the good news. Thank you that you take the faith of believers and save.

DAY 196

Name the pictures and discover your bright future.

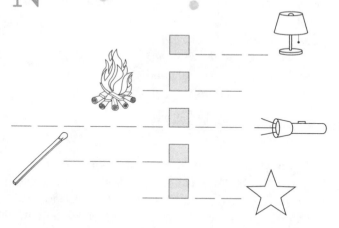

Believe in the _____ while you have the _____,
so that you may become children of _____.

−JOHN 12:36

DAY 197

F.A.I.T.H. Write words that start with each letter to describe your faith.

_____

_____

_____

_____

_____

DAY 198

*Peace I leave with you; my peace I give you. I do not
give to you as the world gives. Do not let your hearts
be troubled and do not be afraid.*

−JOHN 14:27

What's the best gift you've ever received? The world is full
of cool and beautiful things, so it's usually pretty easy
to want something more even if you already have a lot of good
things. Beyond material things, the world offers praise, popularity, wealth, and fame. These things are fine as long as we don't
pin our hopes on them because all of these things we want that
are not from God can be lost. They're not built to last.

God says: "I offer more. I offer things that are out of this
world, things that won't vanish." Specifically in this verse he
names peace. This peace, that surpasses all understanding in
good times as well as in hard times, can't be taken away because
it's given by an eternal God who does not change.

God is our only source of lasting peace. His ways are higher.
His gifts are better.

PRAYER

Give me peace, Lord. When I'm safe or when I'm
afraid, I know your peace is a gift I can hold on to.

DAY 199

May the God of hope fill you with all joy and peace as you trust in him, so that you may overflow with hope by the power of the Holy Spirit.

–ROMANS 15:13

The God of all hope, the God of all joy, the God of all peace is on your side. He is with you always. The Holy Spirit is strength in your weakness, hope in your sadness, and peace in your chaos. You are never alone. You aren't asked to try harder, be stronger, or pretend to be something you're not.

He wants the very best for you, not just what you think is the very best, but what he *knows* is the very best. You just need to invite the Holy Spirit into your heart and then trust. Stay in touch with God, and he will fill up your empty spaces so that you will overflow.

How do you trust an invisible God that is too perfect and too big to even imagine? You simply whisper what is in your heart and invite him lead you. He'll do all the heavy lifting from there.

PRAYER Thank you for giving me the Holy Spirit. I want to trust and am grateful that with this trust comes peace, hope, and joy. Thank you, Lord, for your faithful follow-through.

DAY 200

Finally, brothers and sisters, whatever is true, whatever is noble, whatever is right, whatever is pure, whatever is lovely, whatever is admirable—if anything is excellent or praiseworthy—think about such things. Whatever you have learned or received or heard from me, or seen in me—put it into practice. And the God of peace will be with you.

–PHILIPPIANS 4:8-9

Sometimes the world around us seems like it's only delivering garbage. You don't have to look very hard to find things that bring you down.

Gulp down enough garbage, you'll start to feel like garbage. You may not notice at first. But it gets easier to take in the darkness and participate in spreading it.

But when you're focused on lovely, excellent, noble things, there's no room for garbage. It might not be as easy to find on the news or on your phone, but there's plenty of good, when you look for it. It might be close to home with friends, in the next room, or in God's Word. The first step is to look up and look around for things you're grateful for: sun, strawberries, socks, sleep, good friends . . . You will never run out of things if you take the time to notice and say thanks.

PRAYER

I love that the God of peace is mine and I am his. Thank you for showing me that I don't have to accept all the darkness the sin of this world has to offer.

DAY 201

I know whom I have believed, and am convinced that he is able to guard what I have entrusted him until that day.

−2 TIMOTHY 1:12B

Part of the reason we read the Bible is to learn about our Father in heaven. As you discover more about God, you become more comfortable with his ways.

He's the one who calmed the storm, healed the blind man, loved the leper.

He's the one who forgave the cheat, the soldier, the sinner.

He's the one who died on the cross and conquered death.

He's the one who reassured his followers over and over and sends his angels to say, "Do not fear."

Paul says, "I know this Jesus. He did all these things, especially out of love. So I know I can trust him."

God has given us the Bible so we can know him—know that he is trustworthy. As you appreciate his compassion, faithfulness, love, and power, you can say, "I know the Lord. I am encouraged, because I am his."

PRAYER Lord, I trust you because of who you are. Sometimes I worry, but I'm encouraged that you are always with me.

DAY 202

If any of you lacks wisdom, you should ask God, who gives generously to all without finding fault, and it will be given to you.

–JAMES 1:5

Life can be pretty tricky. Add friends, activities, school, and siblings, and it gets even trickier. Thankfully, God gave us the Bible packed with wisdom and guidance.

What if your mom said cookies are off-limits, but you're really hungry, and there's an extra one that no one will miss? What if you made a mistake, but if you tell a couple of small lies, no one will ever know? What if all you want is the latest, greatest, bracelet that everyone else already has?

The Bible isn't going to answer all of your specific questions, which is just how God designed it. But we have a standing invitation to go to him directly. He will lead us personally through the puzzle of life. What if one friend says something mean about another friend? What should you do? What if your teacher made a mistake, should you say something? What if your dad hurt your feelings? Ask God for wisdom.

God gives wisdom generously. Just ask and wait patiently for his answers.

PRAYER Lord, thank you that I can always come to you. I ask for wisdom from the One who has it all.

SECTION 5

Be Free

Oh I am changed, yesterday is gone

I am safe from this moment on

DAY 204

Think about the many things you love to look at in nature. Write them down here. Keep in mind that there are many reflections of God's goodness found in nature.

_____

_____

_____

_____

_____

_____

DAY 205

"For God knows that when you eat from it your eyes will be opened, and you will be like God, knowing good and evil."

—GENESIS 3:5

The first clue that something is wrong with this statement above is that it comes from the mouth of the serpent. Even though Adam and Eve knew what God said, Satan introduced doubt. The two humans started to question God. Why is he holding out on us? Why is he being stingy? Why can't we call our own shots?

Freedom comes from knowing what to do and what *not* to do. Some actions and thoughts put you right into trouble, but true freedom comes from obedience. God is like the wise, knowing parent who sees problems ahead and wants to save you the trouble.

Instead of eating the fruit, Adam and Eve could have taken their doubts straight to God. He would have received them in love, reassured them with wisdom, and fought for their freedom. Instead they jumped headlong into sin and hiding. Fight for your freedom; follow the Father.

PRAYER

Sometimes I think that if I have freedom, I should be able to call the shots, but that's not how it works, is it? You are God and I am not. I trust you to lead me into freedom.

DAY 206

Follow my decrees and be careful to obey my laws,
and you will live safely in the land. Then the land will
yield its fruit, and you will eat your fill and live there
in safety.

—LEVITICUS 25:18-19

Think about your first day of summer camp. You can't wait to try gymnastics, splash in the pool, or go rock climbing. But wait—your counselor makes you listen to all the safety rules and regulations first, which is the last thing you want to do when you're ready to just get started.

Nobody likes to hear a long list of dos and don'ts. So why did God create the book of Leviticus?

As a new country of free people, the Israelites were new to living on their own. They previously lived as slaves in Egypt and were used to following Egyptian laws. God used Leviticus to show them how to act, live, and treat each other.

Take shopping for instance. The Lord knew that the people might try to swindle each other and get more money than their goods were worth. So he set some guidelines about selling houses, land, and food. He also showed the Israelites the best way to live, like taking care of the farmland so that they would have good crops.

Even today, the best way is to follow the rules, especially God's, so you'll be able to safely enjoy life's adventures.

PRAYER God, rules aren't that fun at first, but I know you put them in the Bible for my own good. You want to bless me with the safety of rules, not make me miserable. Help me accept your guidelines with joy.

DAY 207

These are the words Moses spoke to all Israel in the
wilderness east of the Jordan . . . The LORD our God
said to us at Horeb, "You have stayed long enough at
this mountain . . ." At that time I said to you, "You are
too heavy a burden for me to carry alone."

–DEUTERONOMY 1:1, 6, 9

History is important. It's true. Without history, we forget the important stuff, like the consequences for not doing homework or how stinky our room gets if we forget to put our dirty clothes in the laundry. On a grander scale, countries use history to remember how to prevent war, take care of their citizens, and protect their borders.

God knows that we are forgetful, so he was the first one to tell his children, "Hey, remember what I told you?" "Don't you recall what happened just a year ago?" In Deuteronomy, Moses told his countrymen the story they had just lived: how God rescued them from Egypt, how he led them through the wilderness, how he fed them day and night. You see, the Israelites were already forgetting what had happened. And they were forgetting God. Without the reminder, they may have turned around and gone back to Egypt as slaves. So when your mom—or any adult you admire— says, "Remember?" do your best to recall the past.

PRAYER Lord, often I want to tune out my mom or dad when they remind me of the rules or what's right and wrong. I get tired of being told what to do. But it's important to remember what my parents say and what you say. Will you help me tune in?

DAY 208

But David's men said to him, "Here in Judah we are afraid. How much more, then, if we go to Keilah against the Philistine forces!" Once again David inquired of the Lord, and the Lord answered him, "Go down to Keilah, for I am going to give the Philistines into your hand."

—1 SAMUEL 23:3-4

When David was told that the good city of Keilah was being looted by the wicked Philistines, he went straight to the Lord and the Lord answered. David was ready to go defend Keilah but his army expressed their fear. So David went straight to the Lord again and the Lord answered again. With God on their side, David and his men defeated the Philistines and saved Keilah.

God designed freedom to look a lot like a relationship. David didn't act on his own whims and feelings but went to the Lord. He took his doubts and concerns directly to God and listened for his answer. David was going directly to the Lord he loved, and the Lord answered every time.

Relationships are precious to God. It's the reason behind creation, behind the cross, behind prayer. The closer our relationship with the living Lord, the greater the freedom. That doesn't mean everything is *easy. Easy* is not always *worthwhile*. But grow confident freedom by praying, asking for wisdom, and putting your effort into what God has blessed. That way is always worthwhile.

PRAYER

I'm grateful, Lord, that you value freedom. I want to follow close to you, so I can be free.

DAY 209

As for God, his way is perfect: The Lord's word is flawless; he shields all who take refuge in him.

−2 SAMUEL 22:31

Everyone likes to have some kind of control. You want your room the way you want it. You want to wear what you want to wear. You want to choose what to eat. You may not notice how much you like control until you don't have it. Like when a friend always decides what to do. Or you have to share a room with your sister.

It's human nature to want some control. But it can be a driving force that takes you off the right path. Maybe you start controlling people more than enjoying them. Maybe you start edging God out of your plans because you prefer to make your own plans. Maybe you don't even check in with God because you suspect he'll lead you in a way you don't think you want to go.

Even when you think you must have control, check in with God first. Make sure you're working in the same direction, then your path will be straight, your burdens will be light, and your safety will be in him.

PRAYER You are my Lord and leader. Thank you that I can trust you, come to you with anything, and follow you with confidence.

DAY 210

Unscramble the tiles to find out what John 8:36 says about lasting freedom.

| ETS | IND | YO | EE | IF | U | F | ILL | EED |
| THE | VO | SO | N S | BE | SO | U | W | F R |
| R E E |

S O	I F						

DAY 211

These are things in my life that I need to let God control . . .

_____

_____

_____

_____

_____

_____

_____

DAY 212

I have become a laughingstock to my friends,
though I called on God and he answered—a mere
laughingstock, though righteous and blameless!

−JOB 12:4

When Job complained about a bad day, he wasn't exaggerating! In just one day, he lost all his children, cattle, crops, and possessions. Then Job's body erupted in painful, scabby sores!

Naturally, Job turned to his friends Eliphaz, Bildad, Zophar, and Elihu for comfort. But his buddies—all followers of God—only gave Job more grief. You must have sinned really badly, they insisted. And they mocked him for it. They gave a lot of preachy advice with no offers to help.

Having good friends is one of the best parts of life. They support us, make us laugh, grow with us, and help with problems. Sometimes, however, they can do the exact opposite. Just like Job's pals, friends today can give us "good" advice that is totally wrong, or bring us down with their negative comments. But you don't have to be pinned down with bad advice just because it came from a friend. Before listening to your friends about which road to take, check with Jesus and adults who are wise counselors.

You're free to follow God. His way never wavers even if you can't understand it.

PRAYER Friends are awesome, Lord. But I'm glad to follow you. Please show me what advice is good and what I should ignore.

DAY 213

He reached down from on high and took hold of me; he drew me out of deep waters. He rescued me from my powerful enemy, from my foes, who were too strong for me.

–PSALM 18:16-17

Have you ever gone to the beach and splashed in the water? You can jump in the waves and chase them down. If you time it right, you can body surf and ride a wave all the way back to the beach. Unfortunately a body *surf* can turn into a body *slam* pretty easily. The same waves you can take for a ride can also pummel you into the sand. That's when you get a little glimpse of the sheer power of water.

Even if it's hard to imagine, God is more powerful than a wave that has the power to flatten a pack of surfers. More powerful than a tidal wave that can move a truck. He is complete strength and might. And at the same time he is pure love and care. When his children are in deep, dark waters, he rescues them. He pursues them, finds them, and draws them up. No enemy is too big. No problem is too messy. No situation is too hopeless. God rescues. He saves. He keeps. And he never lets go.

PRAYER I love you, God. You are worthy of trust and praise. Thank you for who you are.

DAY 214

If I had cherished sin in my heart, the LORD would not have listened; but God has surely listened and has heard my prayer.

–PSALM 66:18-19

What are some things that you absolutely love? Your pet? Your parents? A particular movie? Sleepovers? The things that you love can make you happy or sad, excited or scared, because they are important to you. Want to know something wacky? Some people love sin. They love doing wrong.

For instance, a girl at school might try cheating on the next spelling test. She gets away with it. The thrill of cheating and not getting caught could feel so fun that she tries it again on the science quiz. If she keeps the secret and fuels the sneakiness, she can wind up loving cheating. She could actually forget that it's dishonest.

Everyone sins. Everyone makes mistakes. Be careful not to let those actions go unchecked. Hidden sin can lead to *repeated* sin. Repeated sin can lead to "cherishing iniquity in your heart." In the long run, the sin will come out, and the good things you once loved may no longer have a home in your heart. It doesn't make sense to love sin more than your pets or your parents. So stop sin in its tracks.

PRAYER

God, it seems crazy that I could love doing wrong, but I know sin is powerful. Please forgive my sins and help me to turn away from them. I don't want them to settle in my heart.

DAY 215

I run in the path of your commands, for you have broadened my understanding.

−PSALM 119:32

If you've ever been hiking, you know walking a trail is a whole lot easier than stomping through tall weeds. Traveling through wild country, pushing away bushes so you can make it through, might be fun at first—until you get lost or fall or scraped up.

But when someone has gone ahead, found the best way, and cleared a path, you don't have to slowly pick your way through the hard, weedy stuff.

Life has plenty of rough and tangled territory. Without a path and some guidance, you may get lost or banged up. But God himself has laid out a path so you won't get lost among the dangers or bogged down by the weeds of worry. You can move with confidence because someone who knows the way has made a way.

Reading the Bible is a light for the path and the words remind you of the great things God wants for you. As you get to know him and talk to him, you will be able to see the path laid out before you. Sin will look like rocks and thorns you'll want to avoid. His commands will look like a protected trail. Safe in the company of Jesus, your heart will have more understanding and more freedom to go higher and farther than you imagine.

PRAYER Thank you, God, for showing me the way to go that won't trip me up. Help me stay on the path.

DAY 216

Oh, how I love your law! I meditate on it all day long.
Your commands are always with me and make me
wiser than my enemies.

-PSALM 119:97-98

The girl next to you on the bus leans over and whispers, "I love the bus driver's rules. They make me so happy. I think about them when I go to bed at night." Of course that would never happen! No one would say that. So what's the deal with the psalm writer saying that he loves God's law? Isn't that strange?

God's law is more than a bunch of rules. Though there are commands, his law includes guidance for success, wisdom, intelligence, and good life. His law points out the dangers of sin, foolishness, and evil people. It offers protection and help.

The psalm writer recognized how wonderful God's law was because when he followed it, he saw the benefits in his life and got really close to God. Now, does it make sense? You have access to the secret of life—God's law. Once you discover how good it is, you might think about it every night as you fall asleep.

PRAYER

Now I see, God, how your law is much more than a book of rules. It's like the ultimate guidebook. I want to study it and see how wonderful it really is. Will you show me?

DAY 217

Crack the code to complete the verse for lasting encouragement.

When Jesus spoke again to the people, he said,

"__ __ ___ _____ ____
1-0+0   5-2   6-3-1   7-4   139-138

_____ _____, _____
10-7-1   12-10   9-7

_____ ____ ___
1+1+0+1+1   8-2-2   20-18

_____ ____ ___
1001-1000   15-12   11-9

_____, ____ ___
3-0   18-17   8-6

____ ____ ___ ____
50-49   22-20   9-6   777-776

___.
8-4

1	2	3	4
I	in	am	me
of	the	walk	life
but	will	light	follows
have	world	darkness	
never	whoever		

230

DAY 218

Who are three of your favorite people and why? Share how they each have impacted your life on the lines below.

_____
_____
_____
_____
_____
_____
_____

DAY 219

You are my refuge and my shield; I have put my hope in your word.

–PSALM 119:114

This is the best thing ever!" The ten-year-old smiles big at the TV camera. The next commercial talks about a website that helps with school but is also a "great" place to meet friends. Another ad says that if you drink this special sports drink, you'll be unstoppable!

Everywhere we look, commercials and ads try to tell us what will fix all our problems and make life better. Even our friends chime in: "Try this app; it rocks!" or "You gotta buy this song. It's amazing!" They make it seem like you will be missing out if you don't get the next best thing.

Electronics, games, and music can be lots of fun, but they can't fix anything in our lives. Hope only comes from God. He is the one who can fix the bad things, bring us joy, and help us through tough times. No matter where other people point us, the *real* best thing is looking to God to see us through.

PRAYER Lord, a lot of people want to go after the next best thing to fix their problems. I want to be happy with you.

DAY 220

Do not make friends with a hot-tempered person, do not associate with one easily angered, or you may learn their ways and get yourself ensnared.

—PROVERBS 22: 24-25

"You are what you eat," the saying goes. So if you want to become sweet and gooey, eat lots of hot fudge sundaes. That saying isn't really true—have you ever seen someone topped with whipped cream and a cherry? But the idea behind the saying is true.

The people who take up the most time in your life influence you. Some of those changes can be good. Others you may wish would disappear. For instance, just think of the words you've picked up from hanging around your friends.

One way or another, you influence those around you or they influence you. Proverbs gets specific about watching out for hot tempers, lazy attitudes, and destructive ambitions. Spend too much time around them, and those same things will "ensnare" you—turning you into a hothead, lazy, or a bully. When you think of it that way, turning into an ice cream sundae might be the better option.

PRAYER
God, please bring good company my way and show me how to influence my friends for good rather than teaching them my bad habits.

DAY 221

The wicked flee though no one pursues, but the righteous are as bold as a lion.

–PROVERBS 28:1

Getting busted is the worst feeling. When we try to hide something we've done that is wrong, we usually get found out. Sometimes it's a lie we've told or something sneaky we've done.

That's the bad thing about secrets. When we're trying to get away with something, we "flee though no one pursues." In other words, we're afraid of getting found out, so we keep glancing over our shoulder, wondering when we'll be caught.

On the other side is righteousness. When we are honest, we are "as bold as a lion." We are not afraid of being found out because there is nothing to find out.

The best thing to do with secrets of bad deeds is to tell someone we trust, get them cleared up, and move on. Otherwise we'll keep trying to hide. And that gets tiring, especially since God already knows everything we do. Honesty really is the best policy for our own sake.

PRAYER God, will you help me to be honest about everything—even when I do something wrong? I don't want to get in the habit of hiding.

DAY 222

It is good to grasp the one and not let go of the other.
Whoever fears God will avoid all extremes

−ECCLESIASTES 7:18

Have you heard about the most extreme sports? Volcano boarding, train surfing, slack lining (basically a tightrope over a canyon), cliff diving, and zorbing (getting inside a huge ball and rolling down a slope). These adrenaline-pumping, life-risking activities draw people looking for a thrill. As exciting as extremes may seem, the wisest man in the world, King Solomon, said it's best to avoid extremes—though he wasn't referring to sports.

Extremes in any measure push us too far away from what God intended. Here's an easy one to figure out: You love eating French toast. Extreme French toast eating would make you sick and clog your system. Your body would most likely revolt after a few days. Here's a trickier scenario: You love playing the piano and want to become a world-renowned pianist. So you play all day every day. Sooner or later, your fingers will cramp, your mom will get after you to do something else, and your friends will take off.

No matter whether something is good or bad, going to extremes can hurt you. Nothing is exciting enough to risk yourself, your friends and family, or your health.

PRAYER God, some extremes seem obvious to avoid, but I now see how even good things taken too far can cause problems. Help me to notice if I ever go to an extreme and to rein it in.

DAY 223

Daughters of Jerusalem, I charge you: Do not arouse or awaken love until it so desires.

–SONG OF SOLOMON 8:4

What's the hardest part about Christmas? Waiting to open presents! December passes in slow motion as the packages under the tree taunt you. Even many adults can't resist shaking some boxes when they think no one is looking.

Waiting for Christmas is like waiting to grow up. When we see older kids driving, staying out late and dating, we want to experience those fun things right now too. Since time travel isn't an option, we often copy older siblings or friends. We try to dress like them, listen to their music, watch their movies, and use the same phrases. Sometimes that's okay, especially if the person is Christ-like.

Other times, however, growing up too quickly can mean trouble. God gave guidelines to save us from heartache and pain. He knows that trying to act older is like opening a Christmas present way too early. It only ruins the fun for later—not to mention getting you in hot water with the parents.

PRAYER

God, I want to make you smile. So give me wisdom and patience as I wait to grow up all in the right time.

DAY 224

Starting at the arrow, go around the circle to the right (clockwise). Write every other letter in the spaces provided to find out some great news.

John 8:32

_____ _____ _____ _____

_____ _____, _____ _____

_____ _____ _____ _____

_____.

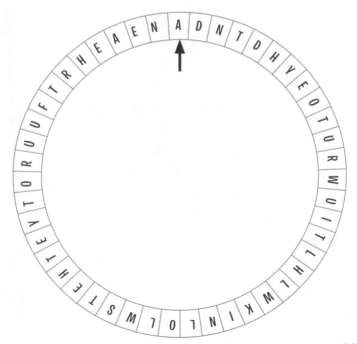

DAY 225

Give God your dreams. Write down a few things you'd like to do when you are older. Thank God that he has good things planned for you.

_____

_____

_____

_____

_____

_____

There IS A *time* FOR EVERYTHING, & A SEASON FOR EVERY ACTIVITY UNDER THE Heavens.
ECCLESIASTES 3:1

DAY 226

When someone tells you to consult mediums and spiritists, who whisper and mutter, should not a people inquire of their God? Why consult the dead on behalf of the living?

−ISAIAH 8:19

The Israelites had seen God's miracles and power over and over. So why would they consult fortune-tellers and psychics?

Think about it this way: If someone promises to give you answers to the mysteries of life or offers to tell you what is in your future, wouldn't you be curious? The Israelites were, just like we would be. The enemy knows it. So he uses his limited influence to deceive people into thinking they can get inside information.

Even Christians in the early church (2 Corinthians 11) had a hard time figuring out who was a false teacher and who was a spiritual leader. The surefire way to know who is legit? Consult the Bible. It says to avoid mediums. That means anyone using psychic powers, talking with the dead, or telling the future. Second, the Bible says to compare what a person says with what Jesus preached. If it doesn't match, then steer clear. Even in jest or "good fun," testing the spiritual world is not something to do without God's direction. Stick with his guidance and trust that if he hasn't given you an answer that you really want to know, it's for your own good.

PRAYER God, it sure would be nice to know what's coming down the road in my life. Help me to trust that you will let me know when the time is right.

DAY 227

The Spirit of the Sovereign LORD is on me, because the
LORD has anointed me to proclaim good news to the
poor. He has sent me to bind up the brokenhearted,
to proclaim freedom for the captives and release from
darkness for the prisoners.

—ISAIAH 61:1

This verse appears at two different times in the Bible, about 700 years apart. The prophet Isaiah wrote it first, reaffirming to God's people that they would be delivered (particularly from other countries). But it also was prophecy, an accurate prediction of something to come—specifically the Messiah—hundreds of years later.

Luke 4:18 records Jesus at the synagogue where he opened the scroll of Isaiah. He read these exact words and said, "Today this scripture is fulfilled in your hearing." What the people of the day didn't understand was God's people were indeed being delivered from sin. Jesus' sacrifice would fulfill the law, open the door to God personally, and break the bonds of sin.

Before Jesus, God-followers had to live up to the law, go to the priests when they came up short, and make sacrifices to reconcile again with our perfect God. But Jesus was the only sacrifice that could fulfill the law forever. With his death and resurrection, our hearts don't stay broken, and we can walk into his light. There couldn't be better news.

PRAYER Dear God, I know what it feels like to lose hope. I know you can speak into my darkness and bring light. Thank you for faithfully offering me hope. I will look for your promises today.

DAY 228

My sins have been bound into a yoke.

–LAMENTATIONS 1:14A

A yoke is a wooden crosspiece that is fastened over the necks of two animals, like oxen. It binds them to a plow or cart so they can pull it. For oxen, it's a farming tool. For humans, it implies severe bondage or enslavement. It's heavy, troubling, and can't be shaken off.

We might think that freedom is doing anything we want, but freedom is actually not being attached even to that want. It's not desiring anything apart from God, because to sin or even to desire sin becomes a heavy yoke we can't control or escape from unless we call for Jesus. Without our Savior, God is judge, righteously punishing us for our sin. He allows us to feel the weight of sin, so that we truly want the freedom he gives.

Don't be fooled if sin doesn't seem so bad at first. It always gets heavy. Go to God before you get yoked. He will always lead you to freedom.

PRAYER
Forgive me, Lord, for my sins. Thank you for offering me my freedom. Don't leave me alone to figure out how to get it. Thank you, Jesus, for saving me from the slavery of sin.

DAY 229

But Jonah ran away from the LORD and headed for Tarshish. He went down to Joppa, where he found a ship bound for that port. After paying the fare, he went aboard and sailed for Tarshish to flee from the LORD.

–JONAH 1:3

God wanted Jonah to go tell the no-good, rotten scoundrels of Nineveh about God's love. Jonah wouldn't do it. He'd run away before ever visiting Nineveh. It just didn't seem fair to give the Ninevites another chance to straighten up. They'd done too much wrong too many times. Can you understand how he felt? God did.

Jonah had the freedom to follow God or to not follow him. Unfortunately he made a bad call. Jonah made the choice to run the other way. Away from God's protection, Jonah headed into a big mess—a massive storm at sea, a three-day stay in the belly of a huge fish, and a long heart-to-heart with the Father. Eventually Jonah freely came back to the Lord.

When you don't understand something that God or your parents ask you to do, talk it over with God. Vent your frustration. Don't hold it in; otherwise you might run away and wind up in a big mess.

PRAYER I know your ways are always best, but sometimes I get emotional and want to go my own way. I know you are waiting for me to return to you. Thank you for that, God.

DAY 230

If your brother or sister sins against you, rebuke them; and if they repent, forgive them. Even if they sin against you seven times in a day and seven times come back to you saying 'I repent,' you must forgive them.

-LUKE 17:3-4

What's the worst thing someone has done to you? Those things hurt. Especially when a friend or family member does it. That pain can last for a long time.

It's okay to tell that person you are mad or hurt. Jesus said the right thing to do is to speak up to the person who wronged you. If you're not comfortable doing that, ask a parent or friend to help you. The hard part comes later. Forgiveness.

Forgiveness means not holding a grudge. It doesn't mean you have to be friends again or put yourself in harm's way. It doesn't mean letting someone else get away with doing wrong. But forgiveness does mean letting your heart and feelings soften toward the person who hurt you. That's tough! Forgiveness means accepting another's apology and also loving him or her even if you never hear "I'm sorry." Jesus said to forgive over and over and over. Know why? If you don't forgive, the pain can eat you up, making you grumpy, angry, and bitter. Forgiveness frees you from all that.

PRAYER Jesus, when someone hurts me, it's hard to let it go. I don't understand how forgiveness can help me. But I don't want to keep hurting forever. Please heal my heart and show me how to forgive.

DAY 231

Use the key to finish the puzzle and find out a couple of reasons why God deserves our joyful praise.

Psalm 68:20-21

Praise be to the Lord, to God our Savior, who

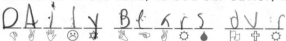

D A I L Y   B E A R S   O U R

_ _ _ _ _ _ _. Our God is a God who

_ _ _ _ _; from the Sovereign Lord comes

_ _ _ _ _ _ _   _ _ _ _ _   _ _ _ _ _ _.

A = ✌   F = ☞   N = ☠   T = ❄

B = ✍   H = 👆   O = ☐   U = ✝

C = 👌   I = 🖐   P = 👉   V = ✞

D = 👎   L = ☹   R = ☼   Y = ✡

E = 👉   M = 💣   S = 💧

DAY 232

Write about a time you had to forgive and a time when you hoped to be forgiven.

_____

_____

_____

_____

_____

DAY 233

Through him everyone who believes is set free from every sin, a justification you were not able to obtain under the law of Moses.

—ACTS 13:39

What if you were invited to the coolest mansion you could imagine? In order to stay, you have to follow a set of rules which include: (1) Don't touch anything worth more than $500. (2) Don't take any pictures. (3) Don't go into the dining room unless you are accompanied by a certified guard with whom you'll need an appointment. *This place is strict*, you think, *but I respect the rules.* Then you peek at the rest of the rules, and the list goes to the floor! You'll never be able to follow all of them.

The Law of Moses was similar. In order for imperfect people to enjoy a perfect God, they had to follow the entire law. It was a super tall order. In fact, it was impossible. People simply couldn't do it, so they would go to priests who would make animal sacrifices (also part of the law) in order to be reunited with God.

Their sin would always be a barrier to the Lord, until Jesus came. Once he fulfilled the law, the barrier of sin was broken forever. It's like Jesus answered the door to the mansion and said, "You've come! Come in! Enjoy! I've made this mansion your home. Feel free to put your feet up and talk to me awhile."

PRAYER

Thank you, Jesus, for taking all sin to the cross and shedding your own blood for my sins. Thank you for satisfying the law and breaking the chains of sin. I'm so glad you did, because you're the only one who could have. I'm so grateful.

DAY 234

But now that you have been set free from sin and have become slaves of God, the benefit you reap leads to holiness, and the result is eternal life.

–ROMANS 6:22

When you're on a team, you wear a team jersey. You're identified by the uniform you put on and the colors you wear. You don't have to declare you're a Seattle football fan when you have the Seahawk logo on your hat. Your allegiance is shown simply by the logo you wear.

When you accept Jesus as your Savior, you claim a place on God's team. You are now identified with God. You're bonded. You are his. The Holy Spirit is in your heart, identifying you as a follower of Christ. He will guide you and let you know his big game plan.

Before you might have been helping call the plays to win. But now you get to depend on someone else, someone who sees the whole board. Your coach and master knows the entire picture and has higher ways in mind. God has the victory, and you are on his team. That's worth cheering for!

PRAYER You are my Lord and master. Thank you that I can trust you and come to you with anything.

DAY 235

*Therefore, there is now no condemnation for those who
are in Christ Jesus, because through Christ Jesus the
law of the Spirit of life set me free from the law of sin
and death.*

—ROMANS 8:1-2

Imagine you are standing in a courtroom. The last conversation of your trial is about to begin. It's an open-and-shut case. You are guilty of sin. You've been convicted, and you wait for the judge to arrive with your sentence. You stand at the front alone. As you wait, you think of your guilt. Sin put handcuffs on you and led you here. The weight on your shoulders is too heavy to bear.

The door opens, and the judge takes his seat behind the bench. He looks at you as you brace yourself for your sentence. "You, Miss, have been pardoned. Your debt has been paid. Your guilt has been put on someone else. But now you have a choice to make: go freely with the one who paid your debt or remain in chains. What will you do?"

What will you do with your pardon? Follow Jesus into life, or stay in chains to your death? You have been pardoned. Live like a newly freed person!

DAY 236

That the creation itself will be liberated from its bondage to decay and brought into the freedom and glory of the children of God.

—ROMANS 8:21

Sin took us out of the garden, out of God's beautiful, original design, apart from God. Now slaves to sin and decay, we are on the "short-term plan" on Earth. The short-term plan involves imperfections in life like brown bananas, shriveled carrots, and moldy bread. Food in decay is not a pretty picture. But neither is a life with sin in it.

The short-term plan gives us a clear picture of what life is like without the saving grace of the living God. The short-term plan makes us long for something better—for freedom, for a relationship with the Father. When we accept Jesus, we can live with long-term plan strength that isn't tainted by sin. That's worth celebrating because when everything is restored with God, it will be better than we can ever imagine.

PRAYER Things that decay here make me long for you and your long term plan. Help me focus on the freedom and glory that is the last chapter of the story, the happy ending in heaven.

DAY 237

You were bought at a price; do not become slaves of human beings.

−1 CORINTHIANS 7:23

Sin has a way of edging into a life, making a home for itself, and then calling the shots. It might start out like a warm fuzzy houseguest, but it gets very bossy very fast. Maybe sin is selfishness you can't get free of, a bad habit you can't break, or a secret you have to keep hiding. But sin always makes you a slave.

What might you find yourself in slavery to? Maybe a "slave master" has snuck in, nudging you away from God and becoming a master over you.

When Jesus was crucified, he took your sins to the cross. He loves you, and you are his. God is your only master. And he's trustworthy and good. Stick with him.

PRAYER You are my Lord and master. Thank you that I can trust you and come to you with anything. Help me spot if I am becoming a slave to anyone or anything other than you.

DAY 238

Use the key to crack the code and find out an important message.

$\overline{}\ \underset{1}{}\ \overline{}\ \underset{2}{}\ \overline{}\ \underset{2}{}\ \overline{}\ \underset{2}{}$

$\overline{}\ \underset{7}{}\ \overline{}\ \underset{6}{}\ \overline{}\ \underset{3}{}$

$\overline{}\ \underset{4}{}\ \overline{}\ \underset{3}{}\ \overline{}\ \underset{2}{}.\ \overline{}\ \underset{7}{}$

$\overline{}\ \underset{4}{},\ \overline{}\ \underset{3}{}\ \overline{}\ \underset{1}{}\ \overline{}\ \underset{4}{}\ \overline{}\ \underset{5}{}$

$\overline{}\ \underset{6}{}\ \overline{}\ \underset{5}{}\ \overline{}\ \underset{5}{}$

$\overline{}\ \underset{4}{}\ \overline{}\ \underset{1}{}\ \overline{}\ \underset{6}{}\ \overline{}\ \underset{1}{}$

$\overline{}\ \underset{5}{}\ \overline{}\ \underset{7}{}\ \overline{}\ \underset{3}{}.$

Galatians 5:1

1	2	3	4	5	6	7
a	is	us	do	be	by	of
it	for	has	set	not	let	that
and	free	then	firm	yoke	Christ	stand
again	freedom	slavery	burdened	yourselves		

251

DAY 239

The best things in life are free. What are some of those free things God has blessed your life with?

_____

_____

_____

_____

_____

_____

DAY 240

Indeed, we felt we had received the sentence of death. But this happened that we might not rely on ourselves but on God, who raises the dead. He has delivered us from such a deadly peril, and he will deliver us again. On him we have set our hope that he will continue to deliver us.

—2 CORINTHIANS 1:9–10

What do you do when you've had a hard day? Do you cry to your mom? Get hugs from your dad? Text a friend or crawl under the covers? What if you got bad news that a hug can't fix or that lasts longer than a day and feels heavier than you think you can bear?

Here's the truth: Regardless of how deep the pit, God's love reaches deeper. No matter how dark the sadness, God's hope is brighter. No matter how long the suffering, God's deliverance is final.

While you hang on to the hope that God gives, remember that he never dismisses your pain. He knows hurt and despair and wraps you in his loving arms. God handles hard days and hard news. He gives us true hope and deliverance. Nothing, not even a sentence of death, is too big. He has already conquered death and he is Lord over all. And you, sweet one, are his.

PRAYER Lord, I cry to you when things get hard. Thank you for comforting me and covering me in love and hope.

DAY 241

Now the Lord is the Spirit, and where the Spirit of the Lord is, there is freedom.

–2 CORINTHIANS 3:17

What if your mom gave you a map to hidden treasure? She buried it herself, so she knows exactly how to get to it. When she gave you the map, she said, "It may look like there are many ways to get there, but there is really only one way. If you study the map, it will take you right to it. If you just go charging out, without a plan, you may waste a whole lot of time looking for the one path." What would you do? Would you take a look at the map, decide it doesn't look that hard to find, and rush to get started? Or, would you study the map so you could find the right way right away?

God has given us access to treasure that our whole being longs for—freedom. As humans we crave it. Countries fight for it. Souls search for it. In this verse above, we are told the way to get it. The way to freedom is the Lord. If you know Jesus, you have his Spirit with you. He is your guide to freedom. We follow him, we find true freedom—freedom on the inside.

PRAYER Thank you, God, that you want me to be free. I invite your Spirit to show me the way.

DAY 242

But the Scripture declares that the whole world is a prisoner of sin, so that what was promised, being given through faith in Jesus Christ, might be given to those who believe.

–GALATIANS 3:22

Maybe you don't feel much like a prisoner, but most humans can't go a single day without sinning. That's part of being human and the curse and hold of sin. Whenever you choose something you know is wrong or decide to do something even though it could hurt you, it's like being a slave to it. There are sins of doing. And there are sins of leaving things undone. You don't have to be locked up in a jail cell to be a prisoner. Being a prisoner to sin means having a habit, a secret, or a wrong belief that has power over you instead of the other way around. The prison can be a desire you have or jealousy that's hard to escape.

But freedom is possible in Jesus. He died so we wouldn't have to be a prisoner. He alone can break the grip of sin. It's not just a quick jump to freedom. The jailbreak is a process. It happens through having a relationship with God. He will lead you the whole way.

PRAYER Lord, I want freedom. I don't want sin to get the best of me, because then I'm like a slave. You set me free, so I trust in you.

DAY 243

It is for freedom that Christ has set us free. Stand firm, then, and do not let yourselves be burdened again by a yoke of slavery.

–GALATIANS 5:1

Sin has a way of making us feel like we're in jail. If you lied to your mom, you may feel sick to your stomach. It may be all you can think about. It may feel dark and scary. You might lie again to cover your tracks or you might just feel brokenhearted. You might avoid your mom while you wrestle with your guilt.

But Jesus doesn't want you to be in the jail of sin. He wants you to be free of worry, shame, and guilt so that your heart can be glad and light. That's how freedom feels. So if we confess and come back under the safety of God's truth and love, he promises joy and light—free to see His goodness, free to give it to others.

God doesn't leave us hopeless in our sin prisons. He opens the door and invites us out. Maybe confession is needed in order to set you free. Definitely prayer is. You may have a consequence from the sin, but you will breathe easier as you deal with it, because you will be walking from cold darkness into warm light.

PRAYER
Lord, only you can set me free from the worry and burdens of my sin. I'm so glad you want that for me.

DAY 244

You, my brothers, were called to be free. But do not use your freedom to indulge the sinful nature, rather, serve one another in love.

It's natural to look out for yourself, but a strength that becomes too strong may turn bad and become a weakness; it can turn to selfishness. But as children of God, we have the Holy Spirit to guide us, and this is better than relying on human nature. So we were called to something greater and better. We were called to be free.

God asks us to look outside of ourselves and care for other people. We are called to consider their needs and perspectives. We are called to see others, listen to them, and treat them with respect.

Sit with a lonely student at lunch, reach out to the classmate who is new to school, include everyone who wants to play, offer help to the one who looks lost. Be cooperative at home, play with your brother, help your mom. Be respectful in the way you talk, be a person of your word whom others can trust.

Look around. Where there are people, there is need. Prepare your heart to see it with a smile.

PRAYER Remind me, Lord, not to get so busy or self-focused that I don't see someone else. Thank you for loving me, and help me extend it to those around me.

DAY 245

Write the words of the verse in the crossword puzzle. (Hint: Start with the longest word.)

When hard pressed, I cried to the Lord; he brought me into a spacious place.

–PSALM 118:5

DAY 246

When I am helping _____, I feel _____
and it makes me want to:

_____

_____

_____

_____

_____

DAY 247

I also want the women to dress modestly, with decency and propriety, adorning themselves, not with elaborate hairstyles or gold or pearls or expensive clothes, but with good deeds, appropriate for women who profess to worship God.

—1 TIMOTHY 2:9-10

It sounds as though Paul wanted the women to look plain. What's wrong with jewelry and stylish clothes?

Fashion was all the rage in Greek society. Women everywhere were trying to outdo each other with the latest styles. Sound familiar? The competition crept into the church. Ladies showed up to church dressed like were going to a prom or an awards ceremony rather than to worship God. The way they were dressing up was distracting others.

There are times and places for dressing up: a fancy dinner, a graduation, or special celebration. Clothes, accessories, new hairstyles, and shoes are fun, but be careful not to let the latest swag overshadow the important things in life. Dress appropriately for where you are going. You will look nice without sticking out or distracting others. With moderation and modesty you can still be a fashionista but without pushing things to the limit.

PRAYER Lord, I like to dress up and express myself. Help me keep it in proper perspective.

DAY 248

[The grace of God] teaches us to say "No" to ungodliness and worldly passions, and to live self-controlled, upright and godly lives in this present age, while we wait for the blessed hope—the appearing of the glory of our great God and Savior, Jesus Christ.

–TITUS 2:12-13

If you knew a jelly-filled donut would make you sick and break out in hives, would you still eat it?

Here's another choose-your-own-adventure to test your willpower: You get twenty dollars from an aunt. You really want to go to a movie but that twenty dollars puts you closer to a being able to buy what you've been saving up for since your birthday. What do you choose?

Self-control—which sounds less fun than scrubbing the floor—comes from learning to count the cost. Why does God care about self-control if he forgives our sins? Is he just testing how much we can restrain ourselves and get stronger? No. God knows that without self-control, we will most likely end up caught in sin and risk turning away from him.

Self-control keeps you on God's path, which will lead you to an amazing reward in heaven one day. Plus, you get to rely on God's strength to put self-control into practice.

PRAYER God, I couldn't master self-control without your help. Too many things are tempting and appealing. Remind me to count the cost.

DAY 249

*Since the children have flesh and blood, he too shared
in their humanity so that by his death he might break
the power of him who holds the power of death—that
is, the devil—and free those who all their lives were
held in slavery by their fear of death.*

–HEBREWS 2:14-15

Would you rather walk into a tree or the shadow of a tree? Shadows aren't scary because they have no weight or power. You can walk right through them. Would you rather face a dog's bite or its bark? The bark is just noise. It doesn't hurt.

Our faith is in the power of the living God. We then, as Christians face only shadows and noise in our lives. With the resurrection, Christ conquered death. So even death is shadow and fear is noise. The Bible reminds us over and over, "Do not fear." If we are on the side of Christ, then who are we to fear.

Remember Psalm 23: "Even though I walk through the valley of the shadow of death, I will fear no evil for you are with me; your rod and your staff, they comfort me." Christ went before us in life and in death, and he walks with us now. We don't take the journey alone.

PRAYER
Lord, I don't want to be fearful, so I'm grateful that the truth is I don't have to fear anything, even death. Help me rest in that truth.

DAY 250

Live as free people, but do not use your freedom as a cover-up for evil; live as God's slaves. Show proper respect to everyone, love the family of believers, fear God, honor the emperor.

–1 PETER 2:16-17

If you could have a super power, what would it be? Flying? Speed? Seeing through walls? What would you use your super power for? Would you channel it for good or for evil? You could ask the same question for all of your gifts: your creativity, intelligence, ideas, faith, wisdom, freedom, power: will you use them for good or for evil?

Peter warns against using freedom in order to sin or cover up sin. When you have freedom of choice, it's tempting to be only thinking of what you want or what your favorite people want. Peter says to remember God and honor him in your actions—show respect, love others, honor the Father. What are other ways you could worship him in your actions?

God doesn't force us to follow him; he lets us choose to follow in freedom. But even as followers of God, the way we live reflects on him as well. The gift of freedom brings responsibility. Keep walking forward, freely, with God.

PRAYER

Thank you for the gift of freedom. I want my choices to honor you. Keep showing me how to do it.

DAY 251

They will wage war against the Lamb, but the Lamb will triumph over them because he is Lord of lords and King of kings—and with him will be his called, chosen, and faithful followers.

–REVELATION 17:14

When you read a long book, do you ever peek at the ending? When watching a movie, do you like to find out how it ends before you start?

When we study the Bible we know most of it has happened in the past. But some of it is prophecy, which tells what's going to happen in the future. In the case of Revelation, the last book of the Bible, we are given the end of the story. So no matter how unstable, unsure, unpredictable things seem in life, we know the happy ending.

The ending victory is the Lord's. The broken will be made whole. The sick will be healed. The slaves will be set free. And instead of riding into the sunset like a reigning tyrant, Jesus, the Lamb, will bring his followers with him. So be encouraged! We are more than conquerors, now and in the future.

PRAYER I praise you, Lord, as the King. Thank you for making me your child. I will celebrate you and the happy ending.

DAY 252

SECTION 6

Be Brave

Don't back down from the fight

He'll shelter you tonight

DAY 253

What makes you anxious? How do you feel and act when you're nervous?

_____

_____

_____

_____

_____

_____

DAY 254

The LORD will fight for you; you need only to be still.

–EXODUS 14:14

The Israelites had just left captivity in Egypt. After hundreds of years suffering in slavery, they were free. But it wasn't really a party atmosphere. The Egyptians had changed their minds about the slaves and decided they wanted to keep them after all. So as they gathered their horses and chariots, God's people started to freak out about dying in the desert. Even slavery seemed better than that.

Moses reassured the people: "Do not be afraid. Stand firm and you will see the deliverance the Lord will bring you today." The Lord was going to fight for them. Their job: Be still . . . Don't take things into your own hands . . . Don't let your fear mean more than the Word of the Lord . . . Don't devise your own plans. God was calling them to surrender to his plans, plans that would confirm his power and demonstrate his love.

When you are worrying or afraid, remember who is in control, hand over the reins, be still, and trust the Lord. While he soothes your soul and fights for you, bow your head in surrender to the Lord who has it all figured out.

PRAYER Lord, I'm nervous about certain situations. So I give them to you and ask you to comfort my heart, give me wisdom, and help me trust. I will wait for you.

DAY 255

The LORD is my strength and my defense; he has become my salvation. He is my God, and I will praise him, my father's God, and I will exalt him.

−EXODUS 15:2

It finally dawned on the Israelites that they were free. They were no longer slaves, beaten, oppressed, and powerless in Egypt. They were celebrating.

The Lord has given us all a chance to follow him into freedom. Sin is always tempting us, luring us, but our heavenly Father has given us the way to freedom. He doesn't just point out what to do and push us in the right direction; he takes us by the hand in his Word and leads the entire way. The same God who led the Israelites to freedom is also your strength, defense, and Savior. He is worthy of your praise!

There are plenty of challenges in freedom, but he walks with you there too. He is the God of all situations. Remember what God has done for you in the past and trust him today. Remember that you are free and trust that he holds your future. Remember and trust.

PRAYER Lord, I can't imagine life without you. I remember all the times you reassured me that you were there. I trust you will continue to be with me.

DAY 256

The LORD said to Moses: "Bring me seventy of Israel's elders who are known to you as leaders and officials among the people. Have them come to the tent of meeting, that they may stand there with you. I will come down and speak with you there, and I will take some of the power of the Spirit that is on you and put it on them. They will share the burden of the people with you so that you will not have to carry it alone."

—NUMBERS 11:16-17

Moses had a big job. His initial job as Israel's leader morphed into a forty-year desert journey. Keeping a million people happy wasn't easy!

So God immediately sent a solution. He chose seventy men to help Moses with the enormous task of leading the Israelites. He then blew so many quail into the Israelites' camp that each person collected about three thousand six hundred pounds of meat. When God says he will help, he means business! God understands when we feel out of breath.

Have you ever felt overwhelmed like Moses? Do you feel like yelling, "This is too hard for me"? We're not meant to tackle our problems alone. If Moses, one of the greatest leaders in world history, needed help, then we do too. So go ahead—ask God for assistance. He will gladly send it.

PRAYER Lord, you didn't create me to struggle through tough times alone. Will you tell me when I need help and show me who I can ask?

DAY 257

Then Caleb silenced the people before Moses and said, "We should go up and take possession of the land, for we can certainly do it."

–NUMBERS 13:30

When the Israelites were on the edge of the Promised Land, the Lord told Moses to send scouts ahead. At the end of 40 days, they came back with a report. They agreed that everything in the land was huge and great. "Huge and great" is good news when it applies to grapes. "Huge and great" is bad news when it applies to people who already live there, who will not give up their land with a handshake and a wave.

Most of the scouts focused on the fearsome people and the difficulties ahead. "We can't do it," they cried hopelessly. Caleb (and Joshua too) saw it differently. He focused on the power, presence, and plan of the living God. While the scouts worried about what they had seen, Caleb had faith in the unseen; he trusted God.

Sometimes it's hard to know where God is leading. He doesn't just shout directions from the heavens and perform dramatic miracles. He usually works in subtle ways. He likes if we have to lean in to listen to his quiet voice. It means we're paying attention.

Caleb was paying attention to God. He was probably scared, but he trusted the God he knew. His faith was greater than his fear.

PRAYER God, I want to exercise my faith, not my fear. I'm paying attention, so reveal yourself to me. I want to follow.

DAY 258

The Lord said to me, "See, I have begun to deliver Sihon and his country over to you. Now begin to conquer and possess his land." When Sihon and all his army came out to meet us in battle at Jahaz, the Lord our God delivered him over to us and we struck him down.

—DEUTERONOMY 2:31–33

God doesn't mess around. When he says he's going to do something, he's going to do it. When he said that he would win a battle on Joshua's behalf, he came in and tipped the scales mightily.

It doesn't matter what battle we are facing. It might be angry bullies, tough temptations, or a goal we've been working to accomplish. If it's something God has pointed us toward, he will do whatever it takes to make it happen.

Bottom line? God fixes the fight. Sure, there might be a battle for a while, but when he says he's going to win, it's never a question. It's like having a direct line to the SWAT team, an in with the FBI, or the cell number of the entire Seattle Seahawks football squad.

You have nothing to fear. No matter what you might face today, you have a mighty God as your champion, strength, and protector. Whatever battle lies ahead, you're not going in unarmed. You have the one you need to win.

PRAYER Lord, you know what battle I'm facing. You know the ones that are headed in my direction. Thank you that I don't face anything alone. You are with me. You are mighty. You are up for the fight and you will win.

DAY 259

Starting at the arrow, go around the circle to the right (clockwise). Write every other letter in the spaces provided to find out what Ephesians 6:10 says.

_____, __ _____

___ _____ _____ ____ __

___ _____ _____.

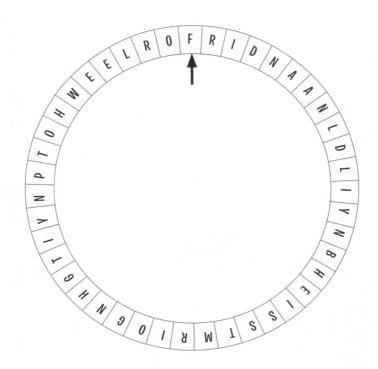

DAY 260

What gives you confidence? How do you feel and act when you're feeling brave?

_____

_____

_____

_____

_____

_____

DAY 261

*Be strong and courageous. Do not be afraid or terrified . . . for the L*ORD *your God goes with you; he will never leave nor forsake you.*

–DEUTERONOMY 31:6

Courage is a rare and remarkable trait. It doesn't come easy. Some people think a courageous person has no fear. But really a courageous person keeps going *in spite of* the fear. Fear doesn't stop them.

This verse inspires strength and courage, but depending on our circumstances, it can feel like an impossibility. Except that courage doesn't depend on your circumstances. *Why* you're scared is nothing compared to *who* is with you.

Think of it like this. If you tried rock climbing with an expert, he would hook you up to the safest equipment and rope. And as you edged off the cliff—the scariest part—he would say, "Don't look down. Just look at me." Same thing here. Don't focus on the fear. Look "up." The living God is with you.

Whether you are afraid of the stage, the dark, or high places, God is with you. When you face surgery, hear bad news, go to a new school, God is with you. Focus on that good news and carry on in courage.

PRAYER It is comforting to know that you are with me, no matter what I face. When I face both ordinary challenges and monumental ones, you are my rock. I want to keep my focus on you.

DAY 262

Gideon arrived just as a man was telling a friend his dream. "I had a dream," he was saying. "A round loaf of barley bread came tumbling into the Midianite camp. It struck the tent with such force that the tent overturned and collapsed." His friend responded, "This can be nothing other than the sword of Gideon."

–JUDGES 7:13–14

Gideon was a little worried. God had asked him to choose men based on how they drank water from the river. Gideon listened and chose the guys who lapped the water like dogs. Hmm. I wonder if he thought that was awkward. *Did God say to take those guys, or the other ones who looked halfway normal? What am I going to do with this crew? I must have heard wrong.*

Those probably were not his exact thoughts, but Gideon did doubt the whole plan. So God told him to sneak down to the enemy camp to overhear how God was going to work it all out. Gideon did, and he overheard the good work God was about to do. Gideon stopped doubting God.

God doesn't often ask us to do what we think will work. Based on Gideon's story, when God asks his children to do something different, God doesn't mind repeating and affirming his plans. We don't have to be afraid about asking God if that's what he really meant.

PRAYER

I am thankful I can come to you and ask for confirmation when I feel like you're telling me something. I want to have faith, but I don't want to do the wrong thing! Thanks for being patient with me.

DAY 263

David asked Ahimelek, "Don't you have a spear or a sword here? I haven't brought my sword or any other weapon, because the king's mission was urgent." The priest replied, "The sword of Goliath the Philistine, whom you killed in the Valley of Elah, is here; it is wrapped in a cloth behind the ephod. If you want it, take it; there is no sword here but that one." David said, "There is none like it; give it to me."

–1 SAMUEL 21:8–9

David was running from Saul. The evil king was trying to kill David, the young shepherd whom God had chosen to become the new king. When David stopped for food and supplies, the priest offered to help him. To the young fugitive's amazement, Ahimelek announced he had Goliath's old sword. Of course, David could use it. After all, that was the sword David used to cut off the giant's head after he knocked him down with a stone. To David that sword was more than a sword. It was a symbol of God's faithfulness and protection.

Do you have something that represents a time in your life when you felt close to God? A picture of your baptism? Your Bible? Maybe a T-shirt from summer camp when you asked God to come into your life forever. Whatever it is, keep it out in plain view to remind you God will be there for you when you need him most.

PRAYER Lord, when you take care of the "giants" in my life, will you give me reminders so I won't forget what you've done for me and my family? Thank you.

DAY 264

The king of Israel answered Jehoshaphat, "There is still one prophet through whom we can inquire of the LORD, but I hate him because he never prophesies anything good about me, but always bad. He is Micaiah son of Imlah.

—1 KINGS 22:8

Wouldn't it be great if every time you went to church, the pastor said, "We are so glad our favorite girl, [your name here], is here. What you are doing is great. You can do no wrong! What can we do for you today?"

King Ahab got that kind of treatment from most of the prophets. Well, except for one. Out of hundreds of prophets in Israel, only Micaiah always had a harsh message. So the king hated hearing from Micaiah. The other prophets hated Micaiah too. One of them slapped Micaiah in the face (1 Kings 22:24) because of Micaiah's message to the king. No wonder the king got upset!

Guess what, though. Micaiah always spoke the truth. He listened closely to God. Everything Micaiah said came true. The moral of the story? When someone corrects you or points out your wrongs, hold off on slapping the messenger. Consider the words. Are they true? Are they from God? God may be trying to get your attention.

PRAYER God, I don't like being corrected or called out in front of other people. But I want to pay attention to anything you say to me. Help me hear you when you are speaking.

DAY 265

No one who hopes in you will ever be put to shame,
but shame will come on those who are treacherous
without cause.

–PSALM 25:3

Because God is who he says he is (faithful . . . trustworthy . . . powerful . . . loving . . .) he is worthy of your hope and trust. That doesn't mean he operates in the way you might expect. He's trustworthy, but he's hardly predictable. He's safe, but he's also an adventure. He's free but completely priceless. He's always good whether we recognize it or not. When following the Lord, you will need to build up your trust in him, pack a little courage, and expect a healthy dose of joy.

Remember this: God is always trustworthy with the big and the small, with the complicated and the simple, with the public and the secret. Follow him and find freedom from shame, pride, and condemnation. Follow him and know love, grace, and mercy. If you don't know the way, start here: "Lord, come into my heart. Show me who you are." Keep your eyes on him and he'll take you the rest of the way.

PRAYER Lord, help me trust even where I don't understand. I want to grow in my relationship with you and follow you.

DAY 266

Write the words of the verse in the crossword puzzle. (Hint: Use the word "the" only once, not three times.)

The name of the LORD is a fortified tower; the righteous run to it and are safe.

–PROVERBS 18:10

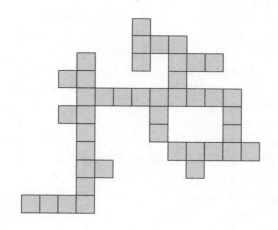

DAY 267

If I could only accomplish one thing for God during my life it
would be . . .

_____

_____

_____

_____

_____

Love the Lord your God with all your heart & with all your soul & with all your mind.

MATTHEW 22:37

DAY 268

The LORD is my light and my salvation—whom shall I fear? The LORD is the stronghold of my life—of whom shall I be afraid?

—PSALM 27:1

In the Bible, God says that even though things here on Earth may feel a little bit crazy, he is with us and he's in control. Over and over again, he says, "I've got you." In the Bible, he shows us who he is, what he values, and what he can do. Whenever we are afraid, or puzzled, we can always go back to the Bible to remind us of truth.

So when someone is mean, remember God loves you. When someone leaves you out, remember you are never alone. When something scares you, remember the fearless one who is with you. When something worries you, remember who can give you peace. When you're feeling unsure, remember who knows your insides as well as your outsides.

Remind yourself of God's promises and truth with the Bible. And then go to him yourself in prayer to exercise your faith and remind yourself of his closeness. God sits above the circle of the Earth. He also sits in your heart. He's got you. The Bible tells you so.

PRAYER God, sometimes I need you to remind me over and over that you are powerful and personal. Thank you for never getting tired of it.

DAY 269

Trust in the Lord and do good; dwell in the land and enjoy safe pasture. Delight yourself in the Lord and he will give you the desires of your heart.

-PSALM 37:3-4

Don't you look forward to a good party? Tea party, birthday party, Christmas party—they all sound fun, don't they? With loads of decorations, laughter, friends, and food, parties are the perfect opportunity to enjoy friends, share stories, make memories, fill hearts, and deepen bonds.

God is not above a good party. He loves to share stories and make memories. He values full hearts and deep bonds. And your relationship with the Lord is worth celebrating. His invitation says, "Welcome! Come in! Stay awhile. I've got some gifts for you in here." He'll inspire you with all of his stories, and you will find you trust in him even more and want to spread his goodness.

You have a personal standing invitation with the Lord. Go to him, share a laugh, fill up, then go out and share the love.

PRAYER Because you love me, I can be confident. Because you hear me, I can be assured. Because you are with me, I can be brave. Thank you, Lord, for who you are.

DAY 270

When I am afraid, I put my trust in you. In God, whose word I praise—in God I trust and am not afraid. What can mere mortals do to me?

−PSALM 56:3-4

No matter how courageous you are, you will be afraid. In fact courage and fear are often present together—courage being the force to go through something despite the fear. Fear is common—fear of the future, fear of rejection, fear of failure, fear of the unknown, fear of spiders. Even in the Bible the first words from angels were usually, "Don't be afraid."

So what can you do in the face of such a common and tough emotion as fear? You go to a fearless, trustworthy God. He can melt the fear with his might. He can strip the fear with his power. He can calm the fear with a whisper. He can starve the fear with the truth. Remember what the Bible says more than three hundred times: "Don't be afraid."

PRAYER

Lord, give me courage. I want to walk with you in confidence.

DAY 271

Trust in him at all times, O people; pour out your hearts to him, for God is our refuge.

–PSALM 62:8

Trust is a firm belief in the reliability, truth, or the ability of someone. The Bible reassures us that the Lord is trustworthy at all times. Have you ever doubted it? Maybe you feel that he let you down by not answering your prayer. Maybe he didn't meet your expectation. Maybe you asked for healing and he answered with the exact opposite. Because we perceive God to sometimes be silent or distant, we may think he isn't trustworthy when really we simply don't understand his higher ways. The disciples didn't understand why Jesus would be crucified and yet that was God's rescue plan for the entire world. To them, it was pure tragedy. Now we can see it for the extravagant, sacrificing blessing it was.

It's important not to rely on your own understanding or worry about what you don't know. Remember what you *do* know: the truth of God's Word. The Bible says over and over that God loves you and he's trustworthy. Trust him at *all* times. He is our safe place; he *is*, right now, present tense.

PRAYER

I trust you, Lord. I'm grateful I can say that with confidence.

DAY 272

It is God who judges: He brings one down, he exalts another.

−PSALM 75:7

Sometimes this world seems totally unfair. A good person will get teased and bullied, while a mean one might get all the respect. Someone cheats on a test and gets an A, while you study all night and pull off a B. It doesn't seem fair when bad wins over good. Why, God?

We have to remember that God has the final say. He sees everything. Even when it seems like he's not doing a thing, he is watching. Often he uses people's sin and wrong choices for his purposes. We can't always see what is going on in God's kingdom. He will make all things right. He will defend the weak. He will catch the cheater or make the bully soften up.

Our job? Pray. Pray for hurting people. Ask God to make things right. And do right ourselves. Bottom line, everyone will one day have to stand before him. Even if it seems like things aren't changing right in front of us, God's goodness is always working everything out for his plans in the end.

PRAYER Lord, sometimes the world seems very unfair. Good loses while evil wins. Please make things right, and help me to hold on to you until you do.

DAY 273

Write the words of the verse in the crossword puzzle. (Hint: Start with the longest word.)

He will have no fear of bad news; his heart is steadfast, trusting in the LORD.

—PSALM 112:7

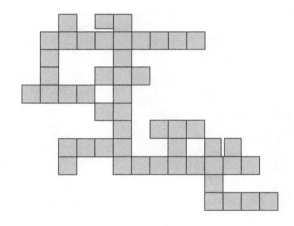

DAY 274

I can do all things through Christ who strengthens me." That means I can:

_____
_____
_____
_____
_____
_____

DAY 275

"Because he loves me," says the LORD*, "I will rescue him; I will protect him, for he acknowledges my name. He will call upon me, and I will answer him; I will be with him in trouble, I will deliver him and honor him."*

—PSALM 91:14-15

Ever feel alone? The truth is you never are. Ever feel unworthy? The truth is you never have been to God. Ever feel faint-hearted, overwhelmed, or crushed? The truth is God rescues, protects, and uplifts. What a blessing that God is delighted to walk through each day with you.

Our relationship with our heavenly Father is like home base. It's our source of comfort and courage. Our part is on the bottom shelf, available to everyone who wants to do it: Love God, acknowledge his name, call upon him. God's part includes things only he can do unfailingly: Rescue, protect, answer, deliver. What a beautiful and unlikely pair, right? Limited, imperfect man and infinite, perfect God, moving through life together.

If a friend isn't very friendly, if a lie has been spread about you, if a family member is super sick, acknowledge your dependence on God. If your future seems scary, if your past is littered with sin, call upon him. Answer every care and disappointment with a call to your heavenly Father. Because you love him, he will rescue you.

PRAYER

Lord, I confess my sins, and I confess my love for you. In joy and in trouble, I rely on the truth of your Word.

DAY 276

I will not look with approval on anything that is vile. I hate what faithless people do; I will have no part in it. The perverse of heart shall be far from me; I will have nothing to do with what is evil.

—PSALM 101:3-4

Previews of scary movies can send a tingle up your spine. Ghost stories can make you afraid of the dark or of any little creak at night. It doesn't take a genius to figure out what is scary and how to stay away from it. Wouldn't it be just as easy to figure out what's evil and stay far away from that?

Evil isn't always outright shocking or obvious. The devil is clever at disguising his ways by twisting good and bad together. That might sound scary too—how will you know?

God's Holy Spirit is like an "evil detector" that goes off inside you. Since evil and true goodness are opposites, God's Spirit cannot mingle with the devil's activities. When you ask to be filled with the Holy Spirit, he sets a boundary around your heart and mind. That way when evil comes around, in any form, you'll know it. No need to be scared. The Holy Spirit is your security system that cannot be hacked or broken into.

PRAYER God, please protect me from evil and help me to know when it's around and how to avoid being lured in by it. Thank you for your Holy Spirit's power to resist the enemy.

DAY 277

*He brought them out of darkness, the utter darkness,
and broke away their chains. Let them give thanks to
the LORD for his unfailing love and his wonderful deeds
for mankind, for he breaks down gates of bronze and
cuts through bars of iron.*

–PSALM 107:14-16

God doesn't mess around. When his people are in trouble and they call out his name, he breaks down gates. He tears off chains. He cuts through bars of iron. He is mighty and strong. You can count on him just like the people of Israel did.

God might not break through the walls of the school, but he might transfer mean kids to another school, change their hearts, or make you stronger to withstand and face them. When you ask God for help, he will step in. He is a protector and savior. You can trust him just like King David did.

When God helps in the way that he knows is best, take time to say thanks. Just like writing a thank-you note for birthday gifts, send a note or call to God. He loves to hear from you.

So ask him, then look for him, then thank him for being so good. Even when things don't turn out exactly as you think they should, thank him for stepping in. He's always looking out for you.

PRAYER Lord, thank you for hearing me when I pray. Thank you for helping me. You're the best!

DAY 278

He will not let your foot slip—he who watches over you will not slumber.

−PSALM 121:3

Have you ever had a bad dream that woke you out of your sleep? Did it seem real even when you woke up? Did you ever go to your parents' room and shake your mom awake just to get reassurance that it was all a dream?

Do you know you can call on God too? You don't even have to wake him up. God hears you as soon as you open your mouth. Actually, he even "hears" you before you call because God is always watching out for you.

He doesn't need eight hours of sleep every night. He doesn't need a nap after sending his angels out on missions to protect his children. He doesn't need to put his feet up after a long day of answering people's prayers. He is ready. Always ready. Will you call on him?

PRAYER God, I don't always think to call out to you when I need help. Thanks for reminding me that you are always there when I need you. Please protect me and help me when I am afraid.

DAY 279

When I called, you answered me; you greatly emboldened me.

−PSALM 138:3

In the Psalms David talks directly to God. Through poetry and verse, the shepherd pours out his heart to the King. Sometimes it's pure praise, and sometimes it's heartache. Sometimes it's in victory and sometimes it's in failure. The psalms show the range of their close relationship—a son to his father, a friend to another, a child after God's own heart.

David's openness is a beautiful thing. And so is God's acceptance. He receives David's outpouring and delights in their bond. David calls out and God answers. He doesn't turn away. He doesn't hear passively. He *listens* with love and intent.

God invites you into the same connection. Call out to him and he will answer. He will give you reassurance, encouragement, tenderness, wisdom, and courage.

PRAYER Sometimes I don't come to you, because I don't think you will approve of my feelings and failings. But I see that David wasn't perfect, and you always welcomed him. I'm coming to you now, O Lord.

DAY 280

Unscramble the tiles. Then write the correct letters in each box, and find out the comfort of Isaiah 41:10.

P V	F O	U A	U P	I	W I T	I W	S M A
F E	I G H	D O	R I	I	V O	F O R	H M
T E O	T R E	Y E D	V R	N O T	I L L	R I G	L S
N D	S O	H O L	W I T	O U	D I	H Y	H T
N O T	D Y	N G T	D O	W I L	A M	H A N	O U
U S	A M	H E L	U R	H E N	A R	D	Y O
G O D	O U	B E

S O						
		D O				

294

DAY 281

Has there ever been a time when you knew God worked out a situation in your life? Write that story here. If not, write a prayer to God asking him to help you with something you face today.

_____

_____

_____

_____

_____

_____

DAY 282

He gives strength to the weary and increases the power of the weak.

–ISAIAH 40:29

You don't have to be an expert putter, chipper, or driver to enjoy the best part of a golf game—the golf cart! Like a swift little speed wagon, it seems almost tailor-made for a kid-size driver. It doesn't even need gas! It does however need a power source. An electric golf cart has a big battery. If it isn't recharged, the speed wagon is at a standstill. It looks exactly the same from the outside; it seems like it should go, but it has no power.

In the same way, it's important to plug into your power source every single day, so you can have the spiritual energy to do God's work. You are the vehicle, but you can't do it alone. If you're not in touch with the Lord every day, powering up, you won't be going anywhere. Remember who alone holds the power, plug in, and then get ready to move.

PRAYER

Lord, I know I can't really go anywhere without your power, direction, and blessing. Thank you for showing me where to go.

DAY 283

How would you feel about exploring a cave you had never seen before? Before heading into the thick darkness, you listen for animals that might be inside. You take a few steps in and strain to see. You duck so you won't hit your head and step carefully so you won't trip. Weird, unexplained sounds pierce the silence. It's completely new territory and yet you can't really take it in. How scary would that be?

But what if a guide offered to go with you? He's been in that cave before, and he knows all about it. He takes you by the hand, because he knows the smoothest way to go. He steers you around rocks and tells you when there's going to be a low ceiling. He explains the sounds. Wouldn't you feel a whole lot better, no matter how dark it was?

God is our guide. He himself is showing us how to go. He knows the way, and he says, "I will take you. I will help you. Don't worry about the bats."

PRAYER God, I know I don't have to be afraid of anything in the past, present, or future. You are with me and you promise to help me. Your presence gives me great comfort.

DAY 284

Ten days later the word of the LORD came to Jeremiah.

—JEREMIAH 42:7

Wouldn't it be cool to call down fire from heaven (1 Kings 18:16–40), send bears to attack mean people (2 Kings 2:23–25), heal the dead (2 Kings 4:18–37), and keep your fridge stocked forever (2 Kings 4)?

Prophets had pretty awesome skills. But they still had to answer to God. Even with their unique job description, they couldn't control the Lord with a snap of their fingers.

Case in point: Jeremiah. When a group of army officers asked him to pray for guidance over their next military maneuver, he said yes. God's answer, however, did not come that night or the next day, but ten days later.

People—even prophets—tend to get irritated or doubtful when God doesn't answer right away. Yet Jesus doesn't always give us what we want, or give it the moment we ask. It doesn't mean he's upset or that we're being punished. Sometimes in his infinite wisdom, he just makes us wait.

No matter what, God hasn't forgotten about you and knows what he's doing. Will you spend the time waiting on him with an agitated, doubting attitude? Or patiently as he prepares the best possible answer?

PRAYER If Jeremiah had to wait on you, then I definitely do too. But waiting is no fun, God. I need faith and patience.

DAY 285

"I am the LORD, the God of all mankind. Is anything too hard for me?"

−JEREMIAH 32:27

People have always had short attention spans. Consider the Israelites. After hundreds of years of slavery in Egypt, they were dramatically freed by God. But soon they were complaining about their freedom in the desert. "It's so hard, and we're starving!" So God sent miraculous manna every single day for them to eat. But soon they were complaining about not having enough meat. So God sent a ton of quail. But soon the people were complaining about thirst. So God sent water from a rock. And on and on it went.

God reminds his people over and over who he is. "Is anything too hard for me?" asks the God who fashions planets, calms storms, and hangs rainbows. Nothing is too hard. And nothing is too small. He's the God of galaxies and also the God of your heart. He cares about nations, and he cares about you. If you have a problem, nothing is too complicated, messy, or ugly for God to make it beautiful. Remember who he is.

PRAYER

Wow, the same God who freed the Israelites from Egypt freed me from sin. I'm glad I get to know you now. Thanks for reminding me I'm in good hands.

DAY 286

So they took Jeremiah and put him into the cistern of Malkijah, the king's son, which was in the courtyard of the guard. They lowered Jeremiah by ropes into the cistern; it had no water in it, only mud, and Jeremiah sank down into the mud.

–JEREMIAH 38:6

Bullied and mistreated. Beaten up and insulted. Jeremiah was a target over and over. But God delivered him out of each situation. When a bunch of guys threw him into an empty muddy well, one of the king's servants wouldn't stand for it. He reported it to the king and went to save Jeremiah.

Some people don't have the strength or ability to stand up for themselves. They can do nothing to prevent bullies from picking on them. If you're in a position to help those who are mistreated, jump in! Use your size, your popularity, your strength, your intelligence to stand up for what's right and protect others who are weaker. You may be able to help another kid figure out how to get out of the bull's eye.

If you are the one who gets mistreated, ask God to send friends who will stand up for you and protect you. He did it for Jeremiah, and he can provide you with a strong companion.

PRAYER   God, I don't understand why some kids are so mean and pick on others. If I have the chance to help someone out, will you help me to do it?

DAY 287

Good is uniquely good. Crack the code and find out what Isaiah 43:11 says about the Lord.

— , — — — — — , — — — — — —
..   . ...- .   -.   ..   .- --   - .... .

— — — — , — — — — — — — — —
.-.. --- .-. -..   .- -. -..   .- .--. .- .-. -

— — — — — — — — — — — — — —
..-. .-. --- --   -- .   - .... . .-. .   .. ...

— — — — — — — — — .
-. ---   ... .- ...- .. --- .-.

A = ._
D = _..
E = .
F = .._.
H = ...
I = ..
L = ._..
M = __
N = _.
O = ___
P = .__.
R = ._.
S = ...
T = _
V = ..._

DAY 288

When do you feel like your most beautiful self?

_____

_____

_____

_____

DAY 289

If we are thrown into the blazing furnace, the God we serve is able to deliver us from it, and he will deliver us from Your Majesty's hand. But even if he does not, we want you to know, Your Majesty, that we will not serve your gods or worship the image of gold you have set up.

–DANIEL 3:17-18

These guys sound tough. But it wasn't because they were just acting tough and talking all big. Shadrach, Meshach, and Abednego had already lost their families and their homes when they were taken captive and moved to another country. As far as we know, they only had each other—and God—to count on.

They didn't get strength and courage in just one day. They had been obeying and praying to God their entire lives. They practiced having faith since they were little boys, and they grew their relationship with the living God. So they were strong before they even faced the furnace flames. Because they knew God so well, these three friends were not going to betray their beliefs. They stuck together. And they knew that, even though they asked God to deliver them from death in a furnace, God might allow them to die.

How solid are your friends and your faith? You know God will stick with you. Will your friends?

PRAYER Wow, God, I don't know if I have what it takes to risk standing up for you in the face of such threats. Teach me more about your awesomeness and surround me with godly friends so that I never doubt you.

DAY 290

So the king gave the order, and they brought Daniel and threw him into the lion's den. The king said to Daniel, "May your God, whom you serve continually, rescue you!"

–DANIEL 6:16

When Daniel was young, his homeland was taken over by Babylonia. Everything was different. The only thing that didn't change was the Almighty God's presence in Daniel's life. This is what Daniel counted on, and his faithfulness caught the eye of the high courts and foreign king.

After some evil trickery, Daniel was arrested and lowered into a lions' den as punishment. When the king rushed back the next morning, he called out, "Daniel, servant of the living God, has your God whom you serve continually been able to rescue you from the lions?" And the king confirmed what he himself had witnessed: "[The Lord] rescues and he saves; he performs signs and wonders in the heavens and on earth . . ."

The rescue from the lions was clearly miraculous. But equally stunning was a foreign king confirming the existence of God and his power. As he watched Daniel's allegiance to the Lord, that same king became convinced that Lord of the Israelites was Lord over all.

God wants everyone to know him. A powerful witness is perfect for showing his love and power.

PRAYER Thank you for showing me, Lord, how you pursue people. Your love and mercy are amazing.

DAY 291

"Come," [Jesus] said. Then Peter got down out of the boat, walked on the water and came toward Jesus. But when he saw the wind, he was afraid and, beginning to sink, cried out, "Lord, save me!" Immediately Jesus reached out his hand and caught him. "You of little faith," he said, "why did you doubt?"

–MATTHEW 14:29-31

As a disciple Peter was on the front lines of Jesus' ministry. Enthusiastic and passionate, Peter was never wishy-washy or neutral in his actions.

Sometimes his first instinct was unfortunate, like when he cut off the ear of a soldier to protect Jesus from the cross. Sometimes his first instinct was naïve, like when he declared he would never deny Jesus, but then did. Sometimes his first instinct was bold, like when he jumped out of the boat to walk on the sea. Jesus had said, "Come," and Peter did. But then he took his eyes off the one who called him. Instead he looked at the storm and the waves. "Save me!" he cried as he began to sink. And of course, Jesus did.

Peter had faith in his Savior. After all, he jumped out of the boat and called to him for rescue. But he got distracted by his circumstances. When he took his eyes off Jesus, he lost his focus, he lost his nerve and his way. It takes brave hearts and minds to constantly focus on Jesus. But he is the Savior. Keep your eyes on him.

PRAYER It is hard to stay focused on you and not the things I feel and see around me. I know that when I get distracted or worried, I can always refocus on you, and you will reach your hand out to save me.

DAY 292

Jesus looked at them and said, "With man this is impossible but with God all things are possible."

–MATTHEW 19:26

In Jesus' day, the culture was full of misconceptions about God. Religious giants knew the law and did their best to follow it perfectly. They had power, influence, and wealth. They thought that if you were sick or poor, then you must have done something to make God mad. It was common to think that the blessings in this life were blessings from God. So if you were wealthy, then God must be on your side, they thought.

Even the disciples were shocked to hear that it was easier for a camel to go through the eye of a needle than for a rich man to enter the kingdom of God. If a rich, "blessed" person couldn't get into heaven, what chance did any others have?

The disciples were still learning from the Savior himself that we inherit eternal life because of what Jesus did on the cross, not because of what we have, what church we attend, what rules we follow, or what we look like. When we follow Jesus, it means we don't follow the culture. We cling to the truth of God's Word.

PRAYER Lord, I want to be brave and stand up to the culture that doesn't understand your ways. Show me how I can be a light for your truth and love.

DAY 293

Jesus entered the temple courts and drove out all who were buying and selling there. He overturned the tables of the money changers and the benches of those selling doves.

−MATTHEW 21:12

Jesus was a nice guy. So can you imagine everyone's faces when Jesus got angry in the temple? People were probably in complete shock.

What seemed like total chaos was actually Jesus displaying righteous anger at what was happening in his Father's house. In those days, God required people to offer animals as sacrifices for their mistakes. Not everyone owned these creatures, so they bought them from animal sellers. Gradually, these sellers moved their mini-markets directly inside the church. Then they jacked up prices to make lots of money. Jesus knew that was not right. So his anger over watching something very wrong motivated him to action.

When you see something wrong, it's okay to get angry—as long as you use that anger to do something right. Following Jesus isn't just about being a nice girl. It's also about following Jesus' example and fighting for what's right.

PRAYER Jesus, show me when I should speak up or stand up, and give me the courage to follow through with truth and righteousness.

DAY 294

Search up, down, and sideways to find the words in the verse. (Repeating words will be found once.) How many times can you find the word *stronghold*?

The salvation of the righteous comes from the LORD; he is their stronghold in time of trouble.

–PSALM 37:39

```
T  G  O  T  E  D  S  H  I  F  F  X  Q  D  Z
C  R  U  R  M  Q  R  V  T  D  H  V  D  Z  C
Y  K  O  E  I  X  E  D  A  K  V  T  T  D  O
A  D  Z  U  T  B  H  S  C  E  P  F  Q  L  M
S  R  W  B  B  M  O  R  F  H  T  P  C  O  E
U  V  B  A  T  L  K  C  F  I  S  N  S  H  S
W  R  W  H  A  X  E  X  H  O  O  G  O  G  M
P  D  E  J  M  B  D  C  Q  I  D  R  E  N  J
H  I  R  W  P  Q  N  F  T  R  G  H  Q  O  F
R  T  C  O  H  C  W  A  P  K  T  A  M  R  Y
U  S  A  O  L  P  V  V  O  R  G  Z  X  T  M
S  N  W  C  R  L  I  R  H  J  T  V  X  S  J
E  M  C  U  A  K  R  G  P  O  X  Q  G  E  M
B  T  L  S  M  R  I  G  H  T  E  O  U  S  V
P  Y  C  U  G  I  E  D  U  M  Y  S  T  T  Z
```

COMES	STRONGHOLD
FROM	THE
LORD	THEIR
RIGHTEOUS	TIME
SALVATION	TROUBLE

DAY 295

God wants you to be bold for him. If you could dare yourself to do anything for God, what would it be?

_____

_____

_____

_____

_____

DAY 296

Do you think I cannot call on my Father, and he will at once put at my disposal more than twelve legions of angels?

–MATTHEW 26:53

Even though guards had just captured Jesus, Jesus could have called down an army of angels. Wouldn't that have been something? Twelve legions of mighty warriors coming down and flying into battle? It would have been a pretty quick win for Jesus.

But Jesus didn't do that. Talk about holding back. He didn't bring in the troops. He held back because he knew he was supposed to be captured and killed. What? He knew he'd be killed so he went along with it? Yes. God asked Jesus to go along with the plan—be the sacrifice—so all humans could have the chance to be saved.

Have you ever faced a situation you knew you could win? Have you ever felt like you were supposed to walk away? If that hasn't happened, it may happen some day. God may ask you to let something go, even when you're right. Maybe someone will hurt your feelings or talk about you behind your back. God may ask you not to stand up and fight. He may ask you to let it go and go along with his plan.

Though it's not easy to know what to do in a situation that seems to be calling for you to make a point, you can thankfully ask God for help. He will help you to either stand and fight, or hold back and let things go.

PRAYER Lord, you weren't afraid to be bold, but you let things go too. Help me to know when I should fight and when I should walk away.

DAY 297

"Therefore go and make disciples of all nations,
baptizing them in the name of the Father and of the
Son and of the Holy Spirit, and teaching them to obey
everything I have commanded you. And surely I am
with you always, to the very end of the age."

–MATTHEW 28:19–20

J esus had been with his disciples for about three years.
They had seen him perform miracles, heal the sick, hug the untouchable, and confront the "stuck ups." The disciples didn't always understand him, but they did trust and love him.

Think of the roller coaster those disciples had been on in the weeks before and after Jesus' death. They saw Jesus ride into the Jerusalem with people celebrating his arrival (Palm Sunday). They saw Jesus being crucified and put in a burial chamber. They saw a huge stone rolled away from an empty tomb. They touched the wounds of the risen Jesus. That is quite a ride! Now Jesus was leaving for good. How could they face everything on their own?

Jesus understood their need for him. He never was going to leave them alone. Even now the Holy Spirit is with his followers two thousand years later. In the heart of every believer, he is God's presence, guidance, wisdom, intercessor, and comforter. What a gift! So as you do the work of the Father, and buckle up for his wild ride, take heart and be brave. He is with you always.

PRAYER

I feel so blessed to have the presence of God in my heart. Thank you, Lord, that I'm not left alone to figure everything out. You are my comfort and courage.

DAY 298

All who were sitting in the Sanhedrin looked intently at Stephen, and they saw that his face was like the face of an angel.

–ACTS 6:15

Y ou have the face of an angel!" Has a relative or close friend ever said that to you? Looking angelic comes in handy when you need to get out of trouble!

Stephen, a Christian in the early church, found himself in trouble. In his case, looking like an angel didn't help. Some synagogue-goers felt threatened by this new, fired-up Christian and brought him in for questioning. Person after person claimed that Stephen said nasty things about Moses and God. Back then, that was a big deal—so big that you could be sent to jail or worse.

Stephen knew that. He also knew the bullies were lying. But instead of freaking out, he trusted God and continued to answer his accusers with wisdom. Stephen also got a heavenly facelift, looking like an angel.

How about you? When you find yourself in a tight spot, can people tell that there's something different about you—something from God? Or do you rely on your own brain, good looks, and social connections to pull you through?

Like Stephen, keep your focus on your heavenly Father. He's got your back—and maybe even your face.

PRAYER Lord, when I go through tough times, I want people to see you in my life. Please make me full of God's grace and power as I learn to share your good news with others.

DAY 299

What, then, shall we say in response to these things? If God is for us, who can be against us?

–ROMANS 8:31

God is so huge, it's hard to picture him. But the Bible reveals his character in ways we can understand, so that we can know and rely on who God is.

Because he has so many parts to his character, he has different names in the Bible. No one name describes him perfectly. He is the Lord God Almighty, The Most High God, Lord, Master. He is The Lord My Shepherd, The Lord That Heals, The Lord Our Righteousness, The Everlasting God, The Lord is Peace. And more.

In Exodus our God reveals how great, faithful, and reliable he is. In his own words: "The Lord, the Lord, the compassionate and gracious God, slow to anger, abounding in love and faithfulness, maintaining love to thousands, and forgiving wickedness, rebellion and sin."

And if we doubted who he was, the Bible reminds us over and over that God is our refuge and strength, a very present help in trouble. He is with us. He is our God forever and ever. How great are God's riches and wisdom and knowledge. He has no beginning and no end.

Go back through these paragraphs and circle everything that describes God. Isn't that good news? This is our God. He is your God. And if he is for us, who has any chance to be against us?

PRAYER

I trust your Word and who you say you are. Make yourself real to me.

DAY 300

For the foolishness of God is wiser than human wisdom, and the weakness of God is stronger than human strength.

−1 CORINTHIANS 1:25

It takes thousands of hours to become a prima ballerina. She starts as a young dancer in lessons and recitals, then goes on to dance in groups in the corps de ballet. She dances every day year round, auditions for prestigious training, and attends a high-quality school starting at the age of 10 or 13.

Does donning a pink tutu make a toddler a ballerina? Would she know first position? Would she be able to take a step in point shoes, let alone an elegant leap in the air? Of course not. The clumsiness of a prima ballerina is more graceful than any toddler. The muscle strength and stamina of a prima ballerina is stronger than any child.

Sometimes humans are like toddlers who get the wrong idea about their own abilities and wisdom. We solve one problem and think we know pretty much everything about everything. Every now and then we need to be reminded that God is prima to our toddler. In every way. Thankfully we can hitch our toddler tutu to God. He has invited us. Don't let the invitation pass you by.

PRAYER Lord, sometimes I think I'm pretty smart and pretty strong. But I would be nothing without you. Thank you for guiding me and giving me courage in your great strength. You are everything in my weakness. I praise and thank you.

DAY 301

Use the key to crack the code and find out some great advice.

___ ___ ___ ___ ___ ___ ___ ___;
  K   K   L   J

___ ___ ___ ___ ___
 J   J   J   L

___ ___ ___ ___
   J   J   K   K

___ ___ –Psalm 27:14.
  L   J

<u>J</u>	<u>K</u>	<u>L</u>
be	for	the
and	wait	take
Lord		
heart		
strong		

DAY 302

Write down the names of God that you know. Then come up with a list of names you would give God based on your life with him.

_____
_____
_____
_____
_____
_____
_____

DAY 303

Be on your guard; stand firm in the faith; be courageous; be strong.

–1 CORINTHIANS 16:13

The Bible is full of godly women who are perfect examples of the qualities in this verse above. Quick-thinking Miriam was on her guard when she saw the Egyptian princess pull her baby brother out of the river. Without hesitating she offered her mom to help care for little Moses. Foreigner Rahab demonstrated faith and courage when she hid Israelite spies. Queen Esther stood firm in the faith when she confronted the king in order to save the Israelite people. And Mary's strength took her on a long, hard journey to a stable by an inn. Each one of these heroines showed combinations of courage, faith, strength, and watchfulness.

These qualities look different on different personalities and in different situations. Courage and strength can be quiet or they can be eye-catching. They can be in public or they can be behind the scenes. They can be frequent or once-in-a-lifetime. But each are admirable qualities that God not only values but provides. Stay close to him, and see what qualities he uses in you.

PRAYER Lord, I see the value of firm faith and courageous strength. Would you bless me with these things in my life?

DAY 304

For though we live in the world, we do not wage war
as the world does. The weapons we fight with are not
the weapons of the world. On the contrary, they have
divine power to demolish strongholds.

–2 CORINTHIANS 10:3-4

You're walking down the street to get a Slurpee when a guy in a yellow suit jumps out from behind a building and says, "Stick 'em up!" while pointing a banana at you. Seriously? No one is afraid of a banana. Who would try to jump you with a piece of fruit?

Everyone knows what a serious weapon is: knife, gun, razor, bat. That's why in movies, the bad guys always carry the biggest, most dangerous looking weapons.

God has weapons, too, but they don't fit with earthly weapons. His weapons are angels, prayer, and supernatural powers. God's weapons are spiritual because the most dangerous enemies are not of this world—the devil and his scheming ways along with fallen angels. Even the most dangerous men on earth are influenced by demonic forces, so when God defeats those powers in the spiritual realm, the guys on earth won't be so dangerous anymore.

When it seems like a problem on Earth needs weapons more powerful than those made of wood and metal, pray. God's powers will go to war in the realm that matters. And one day, he will defeat every enemy and do away with weapons altogether.

PRAYER God, it's hard to understand how you fight against Satan's forces. Thank you for fighting on my side and defeating my enemies.

DAY 305

In him and through faith in him we may approach God with freedom and confidence.

–EPHESIANS 3:12

Think of entering a beautiful palace where you are the smallest thing in the space. At the end of a long hallway is a huge, heavy door leading into a golden throne room. Part of you wants to see more, but you don't know what to expect. Who knows what could be on the other side of that door?

Then the king himself opens the heavy door and welcomes you in. He takes you by the hand and offers to show you around. He has all kinds of good stories, but he wants to hear yours. "Tell me more," he says, smiling right into your eyes. It wouldn't take long to love this king and feel secure enough to tell him your whole heart.

Because of who God is, we can approach him with confidence. By his Word, we can see his heart is good. He has demonstrated his never-ending love and faithfulness. He promises to listen, and we can't say anything that will surprise him.

Go ahead on in. You won't be sorry.

PRAYER God, sometimes I want to hide but with your encouragement I'm showing you my whole heart—the good, the bad, and the ugly.

DAY 306

. . . being strengthened with all power according to his glorious might so that you may have great endurance and patience.

–COLOSSIANS 1:11

The first part of this verse brings up strength, power, and might. What do you think of when you think of strength? Big muscles? Olympic athletes? But then Paul turns a corner and gets to a surprising point. Our goal is endurance and patience. It's like thinking *Samson* and finding out we're talking about *Mary*.

The fact is, being strong is important, especially between the ears. Mental fortitude means having emotional power to withstand difficulty. Implying courage, fortitude comes from a Latin word that means strength. So strength and power do really go together with endurance and patience. To endure a marathon run or a marathon illness, you need endurance. To brave a difficult journey or a difficult relationship, you need patience.

You can exercise and encourage fortitude but God, according to his glorious might, supplies it. Endurance and patience are beautiful blessings of strength from above.

PRAYER Lord, I'm small and slow, but now I see I can be strong. Give me fortitude, show me how to exercise it and make it grow. Thank you, Lord, for providing all I need.

DAY 307

For the Spirit God gave us does not make us timid, but gives us power, love and self-discipline.

−2 TIMOTHY 1:7

A lot of people think Christians are as soft and sweet as jelly donuts. But there's not much to a jelly donut, all sugar and fluff. Was giant-killing David a jelly donut? I don't think so. Yes, Christians fill up with loving kindness, but being a Christian calls for a lot of toughness too.

David killed a giant that sent soldiers away trembling. "The Lord who rescued me from the paw of the lion and the paw of the bear will rescue me from the hand of this Philistine," he said. Elijah faced a hoard of priests by himself and spoke up against the culture. "Let it be known today that you are God in Israel and that I am your servant and have done all these things at your command," he said. Shadrach, Meshach, and Abednego faced a fiery furnace at the hands of a foreign king. "If we are thrown into the blazing furnace, the God we serve is able to deliver us from it," they said.

The source of their bravery in the face of hardship? Always, always, the living God. You'll face your own scary giants, and God will be there. You'll face a crowd and culture that dares you, and God will be there. You will face the heat of hard situations, and he will be there. Call on him.

PRAYER God, with you I can be brave. With you, I can be strong. I feel more confident when I'm close to you. Help me trust you.

SECTION 7

Be One

Why sit around and wait

for a miracle to come

When we can be one

DAY 309

List some ways God has blessed you. How can you use your blessings to be a blessing to someone else? What can you do today?

_____
_____
_____
_____
_____

DAY 310

So the young men who had done the spying went in and brought out Rahab, her father and mother, her brothers and sisters and all who belonged to her. They brought out her entire family and put them in a place outside the camp of Israel.

–JOSHUA 6:23

Rahab was an undercover agent. But she didn't start out that way. She had a bad rap. She'd made some poor choices in life. But when she met the spies from Israel and heard about God, she wanted to change her ways. Good thing the spies didn't ignore her just because of her past mistakes. Rahab wound up helping the spies and all of Israel. In turn, they saved her and her family from destruction; she even became part of Jesus' family line!

Have you met people who have bad reputations? It'd be easy to avoid those kinds of people. But what you don't know is that those kids may not have a mom or dad. Or they might have a lot of stress at home. God doesn't avoid those people. Neither should you. God uses anyone, and he gives everyone many chances to hear about him. Instead of hearing about another person's mistakes and judging them, ask God to help you befriend them. Who knows, you might wind up helping a future undercover agent, the future president, or the next Olympic athlete.

PRAYER
God, it's hard to like kids who cause trouble or seem mean. But you love them. Please keep me from judging others. May I see them the way you see them, as your children with a future.

DAY 311

*They mourned and wept and fasted till evening for
Saul and his son Jonathan, and for the army of the
Lord and for the nation of Israel, because they had
fallen by the sword.*

−2 SAMUEL 1:12

Imagine the First Lady asks you to play piano to cure her insomnia. Your serenades work, earning you her trust and a job assisting other leaders with special projects. Now people want to see you on TV more than the First Lady. The First Lady gets so jealous and suddenly wants you dead!

This is what David went through with King Saul. So after Saul died, David actually felt sorry that the guy who tried to kill him was gone? Shouldn't he have been psyched and happy?

As a mortal man, David wanted to live. But he was also heartbroken that Saul had made so many wrong choices. In the end, those bad decisions cost Saul his throne, family, and life while leading Israel away from their faith.

What about you? When your enemies crash and burn, do you celebrate? As sinful humans, it's normal to feel excited when someone we dislike gets a bad grade, misses the big shot, or lands in detention. Yet that's not what God wants.

Instead of cheering for our adversaries' defeats, will you pray for their salvation?

PRAYER

I want to look at people the way you do, Lord. Help me see beyond bad behavior. When I do, I know I'll find someone who needs you, just like me.

DAY 312

*Let's make a small room on the roof and put in it a bed
and a table, a chair and a lamp for him. Then he can
stay there whenever he comes to us.*

–2 KINGS 4:10

A family in Shunem liked having Elisha visit their home whenever he came through town. In fact, they added a guest room just for him. They gave him a place to stay, and they got something out of the deal too. When he was with them, the family received blessings from God. It was very special to spend time with this man of God and learn from him.

We don't hear of prophets visiting people nowadays. But missionaries often travel around the country to visit churches and their supporters. Check with your parents about inviting a visiting missionaries to stay overnight or come for dinner. Then join in showing hospitality to your guests by helping prepare dinner, making a bed for them to sleep in, or cleaning the house.

When they arrive, you won't only help them out, you'll receive a blessing too. Often missionaries live in a faraway place among people quite different from you. The amazing-but-true stories told around the table or in the family room will blow your socks off. Ask them what God is doing in their country with children your age and how you can pray for them. Who knows, your family might just set aside a special room in the house for missionaries to come any time.

PRAYER Lord, I want to learn from those heroes of the faith that come to my church. I want to welcome them into my home.

DAY 313

At that time Marduk-Baladan son of Baladan king of Babylon sent Hezekiah letters and a gift, because he had heard of Hezekiah's illness.

–2 KINGS 20:12

What makes you feel better when you're sick? A long nap? Hot soup? Lying on the couch with your mom or dad? A day off from school? Lots of blankets and pillows piled around you?

King Hezekiah got so sick that he almost died. When another king heard about it, he sent gifts, notes, and visitors to cheer up Hezekiah. Though the gifts came as a way to spy on King Hezekiah, he ended up feeling better. That's how powerful kindness can be.

Who do you know who needs some cheering up? Instead of using kindness to trick someone, use it to make their day a little better. Unfortunately, on Earth there is no way to stop sickness or cure all diseases. But kindness and thoughtfulness can ease the pain. Visit someone at the hospital, tell a few jokes, or make special food to take to a loved one who is sick. Though their bodies may not heal any faster, your care will make them feel better.

PRAYER

Lord, who needs some care right now? Please show me how I can help them and make them feel better.

DAY 314

Hilkiah the priest, Ahikam, Akbor, Shaphan and
Asaiah went to speak to the prophet Huldah, who was
the wife of Shallum son of Tikvah, the son of Harhas,
keeper of the wardrobe. She lived in Jerusalem, in the
New Quarter.

—2 KINGS 22:14

Don't let anyone put you down because you're a young woman. As you read the Bible this year, you will see that God uses men *and women* to instruct his people. For example there were Miriam, Esther, and Deborah. There was also a woman by the name of Huldah. Her husband Shallum was called a "keeper of the wardrobe." Most likely that meant he was in charge of the special clothes worn by the priests or those in the king's palace.

Shallum had an important job. But his wife Huldah's job was even more important. She was a prophet. The Lord gave her special knowledge to share with the king. In other words, she spoke for God.

You've probably watched women as teachers and leaders at school and church, and older girls helping out with youth group or sports teams. Let the women who have helped you grow in faith know that you appreciate them. Send a text or email telling them how God is using them to help you grow into a confident person of faith.

PRAYER Lord, I am so grateful for the "Huldahs" in my life. I can't wait to see how you will use me to help others grow in their faith. I'm available.

DAY 315

Psalm 91:2 explains why we can go into the world with confidence. Unscramble the tiles. Write the correct letters in each box, and find out what it says.

Y O	D H	D I	R T R	Y R	I	A N D	N W
S A	H O M	G E	~~I W~~	E F U	~~G O~~	S M	M Y
E I	I L L	F O	S T	L O R	T R U	H E	M Y
E S S	F T						

I W							
			G O				

DAY 316

I am thankful for . . .

_____
_____
_____
_____
_____

DAY 317

All these were fighting men who volunteered to serve in the ranks. They came to Hebron fully determined to make David king over all Israel. All the rest of the Israelites were also of one mind to make David king.

–1 CHRONICLES 12:38

Everyone knows David was one of the best kings Israel ever had. Even before he was king, though, the soldiers and all the people agreed to make David king.

Imagine everyone in our country voting for the same president. It would never happen. Or how about your classroom? How likely is it that you could get all your classmates to vote for the same kind of pizza for a party?

Try this: Count how many disagreements you hear at home, in school, or at a game. Disagreements happen all the time. When it comes to important issues, agreement brings people together. That's why in elections only a few candidates get to run for office. The candidates find out what is most important to a large number of people and bring them together on those issues. But disagreements don't have to be negative. You can disagree with friends and family and leaders but still respect them and obey them. That's a big move, but it's the kind of move that could bring more people together one day. With God's blessing, David was able to make it work.

PRAYER God, disagreements always seem so negative. I'm not sure I even understand how a disagreement could be respectful and nice. But I would love to learn how to do that. Will you show me?

DAY 318

I had not been sad in his presence before, so the king asked me, "Why does your face look so sad when you are not ill? This can be nothing but sadness of heart."

—NEHEMIAH 2:1-2

Nehemiah the prophet had been given very sad news. His hometown of Jerusalem had been destroyed, and buildings had been burned to the ground. To make matters worse, Nehemiah was several hundred miles away and couldn't do anything to help. As he reported for work in the palace, the king could tell something was bothering Nehemiah. One look at the prophet's face and his majesty knew there was a problem.

Did you know that your face is a window into your heart? That's the way God made you. When you are happy, your mouth turns up in a smile. When you are excited, there is a twinkle in your eyes. When you are sad, your eyebrows droop and your lips stick out or turn down. Facial expressions create a kind of built-in honesty. You can't really hide how you feel.

Words aren't always necessary. By looking at our faces, our friends and family know how to respond to us. They can rejoice with us, grieve with us, or try to encourage us. And by looking at the faces of others, we can respond to what they need too.

PRAYER Lord, help me take my eyes off myself. As I look into the faces of others, allow me to see what those around me are feeling so I can encourage them.

DAY 319

[Nehemiah] said: "As far as possible, we have bought back our fellow Jews who were sold to the Gentiles. Now you are selling your own people, only for them to be sold back to us!" They kept quiet, because they could find nothing to say. So I continued, "What you are doing is not right."

–NEHEMIAH 5:8-9

Are you shocked or glad when someone gets confronted? "Knock it off," a teacher says to the student next to you. "Hold on a minute!" your dad calls to your sibling. "Guilty," a judge proclaims.

God raises leaders and people of authority so that we don't run all over each other. Leaders have a special role to provide justice—righting wrongs, punishing wrongdoing, keeping the rules in place to protect everyone.

Nehemiah was a leader while his country was rebuilding. They had been in captivity for many years, so they were thrilled to go home. But it didn't take long before some of the Israelites started mistreating each other. Nehemiah stepped in.

Though it's no fun being the one who gets corrected, listening to the leaders in your world will keep you and everyone else safe and in line. It may not seem like a big deal at school or at home, but no one wants to grow up in a world without justice.

PRAYER

God, I'll pray for the leaders in my life. Will you teach me to be respectful in what I say and how I obey?

DAY 320

Dispatches were sent by couriers to all the king's
provinces with the order to destroy, kill and annihilate
all the Jews—young and old, women and children—on
a single day, the thirteenth day of the twelfth month,
the month of Adar, and to plunder their goods.

—ESTHER 3:13

D o you know a soldier who went to war in Iraq or Afghanistan? It's hard when people are sent off to war because you don't know if they will come back. War has happened ever since Cain killed his brother Abel. (See Genesis 4.) Anger (such as Haman's anger about Mordecai), vengeance, power, jealousy (see Esther 3:2–5) lead people to do awful things, including fighting and killing.

Though death doesn't surprise God, he values every life. Each person is precious to him. So during wartime, God often calls individuals to work hard to stop wars and fights.

In Esther's time, she was able to save the Israelites. Her story is one that ends well. She and her uncle listened to God and risked their own lives to save many others. Though Jesus says that death will not end until he comes back to Earth, we can pray against killing and stand up for life.

PRAYER Lord, please protect soldiers who are fighting for freedom and justice all over the world. Raise up people who will stand up to stop wars and fighting.

DAY 321

He who despises his neighbor sins, but blessed is he who is kind to the needy.

–PROVERBS 14:21

Sometimes it's easier to be kind to a stranger than to the ones closest to us. We don't know a stranger's bad habits; we don't have any old arguments; they aren't around enough to bother us. But it's important to show love, even when it's tough. Loving those that rub us the wrong way is important. It helps us grow in our relationship with God because we are obeying him instead of harboring sin and bitterness. It's not always the easiest thing to show our neighbor God's love with forgiveness and grace but it is always the best.

Being kind to *everyone* is a great way to show God's love. He loves everyone and sees great worth in all people. Practice showing respect to a friend who you disagree with, a substitute teacher, a sibling, a food server, the president, and a person asking for money on the street. Kindness and respect cost nothing and yet are precious and priceless, so pass them on.

PRAYER Lord, help me love the needy and my neighbor equally. Sometimes it's hard, but you make a way. Help me be sensitive to it.

DAY 322

Search up, down, and sideways to find the words in the verse below.

Therefore, my dear brothers and sisters, stand firm. Let nothing move you. Always give yourselves fully to the work of the Lord, because you know that your labor in the Lord is not in vain.

–1 CORINTHIANS 15:58

```
X S V C T X Z S E G I S G K W M T D H U
I S C I O D I H R H Q M I B T L M I N V
K E P U N S O T R H T P Q S D T W D D Q
W V K S S Y A W L A B W G K T N N T S K
O L P M O D B R M X G O S Q W E I C C F
Q E L J N L X U G Q L N V D Z V R Z H B
E S B R O T H E R S L K L A F U S S E N
H R T P B J O F D Q S B W N V E D C E X
M U D L P V G X V J Y F B D G U A R G I
N O P Q L V B L Q R V T G B P U O S F P
O Y M O J K Q V U M K I P L S F D X J P
T F E V I Q Q H W F V E V E E C O R M L
H K I U O Y L T O E R T W R Y O U R O Z
I G A R K W A M S O D B E U L V L L V L
N D F M M H L E B Y W H D I L E A B E D
G W N I T E V A Q K T E H P U Y M I S I
S K G A T A L F J G R N Y N F F W D N L
K R O W T Y M D I C S R H U H J B C X Y
E O E N Q S S L S I B J J F C K D E A R
Z J V Q D P K V J W V T B Q J W T S T Z
```

ALWAYS	FIRM	LET	SISTERS	VAIN
AND	FULLY	LORD	STAND	WORK
BECAUSE	GIVE	MOVE	THAT	YOU
BROTHERS	KNOW	NOT	THE	YOUR
DEAR	LABOR	NOTHING	THEREFORE	YOURSELVES

DAY 323

Write down 10 things about God and the Bible that make you smile.

_____
_____
_____
_____
_____
_____
_____
_____
_____
_____
_____

DAY 324

The tongue of the wise adorns knowledge, but the mouth of the fool gushes folly . . . The soothing tongue is a tree of life, but a perverse tongue crushes the spirit.

–PROVERBS 15:2, 4

One simple trick can make you seem as smart as a physicist or as dumb as a fence post. The trick? The words you say and your timing in saying them.

Think about this: When you get bad news, whom do you talk to? You probably call or text your best friend, your mom, or maybe a youth group leader. You probably don't call the school gossip. You definitely wouldn't want to talk to a selfish person or the neighborhood know-it-all who would either tell you it's not a big deal or share the news and laugh.

Words pack a punch. People who choose their words carefully come across smarter. And those people are the ones others want to be around. When you learn to say the right words at the right time, you're being wise. The same is true when you zip your lips during those moments when the wrong words come to mind. Think about what you would want someone to say to you. Then speak like that, a help in times of trouble.

PRAYER Lord, thank you for the friends who speak kindly and know exactly what to say when I need it. I want to be that kind of friend too.

DAY 325

A sluggard buries his hand in the dish; he will not even bring it back to his mouth! . . . Sluggards do not plow in season; so at harvest time they look but find nothing.

–PROVERBS 19:24, 20:4

Can you imagine someone so lazy that she reaches out her hand to grab a piece of pizza for lunch but can't bring herself to pick up the slice and eat it? How about someone so lazy that she doesn't want to exhaust herself by pushing the buttons on the remote control to change the TV channel? "Oh well, guess it'll be a day of the natural history channel." She might as well be unconscious. While you most likely won't meet anyone that lazy, Proverbs has a lot to say about laziness, or slothfulness. Plain and simple—avoid it.

Laziness—which is not to be confused with *rest*—always leads to problems. For instance, if a student didn't read her textbooks, do any of her homework, or listen to her teachers, when the test comes, she will fail. If she remains lazy, she will fail again. Then she won't pass onto the next grade. She may never graduate high school. She likely won't get a job or earn money and will live in her parents' basement until she's fifty!

Laziness slows you down. Little by little. If you give it a small place in your life, eventually it could keep you on the couch for years. Without any pizza or TV.

PRAYER God, I do enjoy a break on the weekends. Thank you for the chance to rest. Will you teach me the difference between rest and laziness?

DAY 326

Whoever shuts their ears to the cry of the poor will also cry out and not be answered.

−PROVERBS 21:13

How many families do you know who don't have enough money to buy food and clothing or pay for a place to live? Though poverty in America exists, most families can get help from churches, charities, and the government. But around the world, over nine hundred million people go hungry every day. Many children your age die because they don't get enough food. Without enough food, they don't get enough vitamins and nutrients to keep their bodies healthy and growing. Often these children don't have electricity and clean running water either.

This kind of poverty makes God sad. When he sees people who don't have enough to eat or drink or a bed to lie down on, his heart breaks. That's why the Bible includes so many verses like this one about caring for the poor. God wants his followers to care for the poor.

Talk to your parents about how you can help poor people in your community or in another part of the world. You might be able to donate the clothes you've outgrown, send money for food, or pack gift boxes at Christmas time. Doing so will cheer God's heart.

PRAYER Lord, I don't know what it's like to be so poor that I don't get enough to eat. It must be a terrible feeling. How can my family help out those who have nothing?

DAY 327

The craving of a sluggard will be the death of him, because his hands refuse to work. All day long he craves for more, but the righteous give without sparing.

−PROVERBS 21:25-26

Summer vacation is one of the best ideas ever. No homework, report cards, alarm clocks, or cafeteria casseroles! Instead, summer means sleeping late, family vacations, and hanging out with friends.

God loves it when we have a good time and rest. In fact, he "invented" taking a break when he rested on the seventh day after making the universe. So he knows what it's like to take a breather.

Yet it's possible to take the "summer vacation" concept too far. The writer of Proverbs 21 called these people "sluggards." That word means constantly inactive and lazy, literally like a slow-moving slug. Gross!

A sluggard avoids work at all costs and never finds satisfaction with what she has. She wants everything right, but wants someone else to do the tough stuff.

So which would you rather be: a lazy slug who always wants more? Or a carefree, hard-working follower of God who always has enough not only for yourself, but also for everyone around you?

PRAYER Jesus, give my hands and heart the desire to work for you. If I am being lazy, please help me change. May my "craving" (vs. 25) to please you bring life to me and those around me.

DAY 328

An honest answer is like a kiss on the lips.

-PROVERBS 24:26

B ack in Solomon's day, kisses were like hugs and handshakes. People kissed each other as a sign of respect, friendship, and reverence. People wanted to be kissed; it was like saying, "You're pretty cool. I'm glad I know you."

Answering honestly says the same thing. It shows that you respect someone enough to tell the truth even when it is hard. Or when you know they won't like the answer.

The truth is refreshing and comforting. When you are honest, the person talking to you doesn't have to guess how you feel. She doesn't have to wonder if you were tiptoeing around her feelings. Even if honesty means that you say, "I'm sorry, but I'm not comfortable answering that question," you've treated someone with kindness.

Here's an experiment: Tell your parents or your close friends that you want to practice honesty. Then tell them to ask you hard questions. Answer truthfully, then ask how you could present the truth in a gentler way. If you already practice honesty, then practice speaking with kindness or restraint. Instead of saying, "Your shirt is ugly" say, "I like some of your other shirts better." In the long run, friends and family will trust you and respect you for the truth.

PRAYER God, I like it when my friends are honest with me, but I'm not always prepared for it. I'd like to learn how to be honest in a nice way.

DAY 329

When we grow in God, we develop qualities that come from him. Galatians 5:22–23 lists the fruit of the Spirit. Write them out here.

1 __ __ __
__ 2 __
__ 3 __ __ __
4 __ __ __ __ 5 __ __ __ __ __
__ 6 __ __ __ __ __ __
__ __ __ 7 __ __ __ __
__ __ __ __ 8 __ 9 __ __ __ __ __
__ __ __ 10 __ __ __ __ __ __
11 __ __ __ - __ __ 12 __ __ __ __

Now fill in the letters that go with the numbers. When you are finished, you will confirm why we can be confident.

PSALM 33:5

For the word of the Lord is right and true; __ __   __ __
                                             8 3   6 11

__ __ __ __ __ __ __ __   __ __   __ __   __   __ __
4 5 6 10 8 4 9 1   6 12   5 1   1   8 3

__ __ __ __.
7 2 3 11

DAY 330

What does having God's unconditional love mean to you?

_____

_____

_____

_____

_____

_____

DAY 331

Learn to do right; seek justice. Defend the oppressed.
Take up the cause of the fatherless; plead the case of
the widow.

−ISAIAH 1:17

Sometimes we think widows (women whose husbands have died) and orphans (children whose parents have died) live far away. You might picture old women in some village or hungry little children in Ethiopia or Haiti. Yes, people do need help in faraway countries, but people need help in this country too.

A widow may live in your neighborhood, or several kids at school may not have a dad at home. Did you know that you can care for them? Jesus wants us to love people, and it doesn't have to be hard. Rake leaves for the neighbor, or invite a friend over for dinner. Bring an orphan school shopping with you and your parents, or take cookies to a widow.

If you are the one without a dad or mom, God notices. He cares. Ask him for help and friends who will care for you. He will send people to help.

God loves every one of us. If we can help, we should. If we need help, we can ask for it and people will come our way too.

PRAYER Lord, I want to help people. Please show me who needs my help today.

DAY 332

In that day the Lord will punish the powers in the heavens above and the kings on the earth below.

–ISAIAH 24:21

By now you've learned that God is love and everything he does is good. So does it seem confusing that he would destroy anything? Isaiah's writings were all about prophecy, or messages from God about the future. Many of Isaiah's prophecies came true when Jesus Christ came to earth. But some of Isaiah's words are still to happen.

Yes, God is loving and good. That's why he has sent prophecies and messages and missionaries to the world. He gives everyone many opportunities to repent of sin, accept his forgiveness, and turn their lives over to God's side. Sadly, many people will not do that. They will hate God, stay in their sin, and never accept his salvation. Darkness, pain, sadness, and sin destroy people and the world God created. That breaks God's heart. In the end, because God is good and loves everyone, he will put an end to all those things and kick evil out of his world.

PRAYER God, now I understand how your goodness and love cannot stand to let evil continue to destroy your world. Use me to bring your message of salvation to people.

DAY 333

I prayed to the LORD my God and confessed: "LORD, the great and awesome God, who keeps his covenant of love with those who love him and keep his commandments, we have sinned and done wrong. We have been wicked and have rebelled; we have turned away from your commands and laws."

–DANIEL 9:4-5

D aniel was one of the godliest men in Babylon.
So what's up with his prayer in chapter 9? He confesses the sins of Jerusalem, but he doesn't say, "Lord, my country has blown it."

Today's world is pretty similar to Jerusalem and Babylon. Countries that began by following God have pulled a one-eighty, completely turning from him. So chances are that your community desperately needs a prayer warrior like Daniel.

If you need inspiration, pray Daniel's words over your country. Tell God where you need improvement and what you're thankful for. Most important, pray for your country regularly. You never know when your ripple could grow into a world-changing wave.

PRAYER Lord, Daniel faced a tough situation. Yet he didn't give up. I want to be like that. Will you give me that same humility and perseverance to pray for my country?

DAY 334

In the same way, let your light shine before others, that
they may see your good deeds and glorify your Father
in heaven.

–MATTHEW 5:16

Have you ever seen the spotlights used at grand openings or special events? Heavy, huge, and powerful, they're wheeled to the entrance of a movie premiere or event. Then they're turned on and pointed up. The gigantic beams of light shine into the night sky. As they rotate and swivel, the beams cross back and forth and can be seen for miles. The idea is to get people's attention so they will follow the light and end up at the event.

When you shine your light before others, you attract them to something bigger. When they see gracious, loving behavior, when they see you helping out or including people, they are attracted to your driving force—the Father. If you're the opposite (if you're snobby, disrespectful, ugly to others) the light is turned off, and no one can see the Father clearly. Wouldn't you rather be full of light for the Father?

God's light is already working in you. Shine the faithfulness and joy that he shows to you on to others. Let it show through your actions and expressions.

PRAYER

Thank you, Lord, for your light in my life. I'm happy to shine it so it reflects back to you.

DAY 335

. . . just as the Son of Man did not come to be served, but to serve, and to give his life as a ransom for many.

−MATTHEW 20:28

At first glance, the term "servant leader" seems like a nonsensical notion of two opposites. But actually a servant leader is one who guides with others in mind. He uses humility and trust to blend service with leadership. Today a lot of people climb the corporate ladder, step on people to get to the top, and obsess about getting beyond the glass ceiling. But servant leadership is the opposite.

Maybe you've heard of Mother Teresa. She didn't care about being well-known. She cared about the poorest of the poor. She cared for the unwanted and hopeless in Calcutta, India. Without arrogance or self-importance, she led aid workers in her goal to serve the Lord and help others.

Jesus was the ultimate servant leader. He wasn't self-motivated but self-sacrificing. He wasn't out for profit or personal glory but for the Father. The only one on earth who deserved to boast about his greatness actually focused on others—his disciples, the needy, his followers, and the lost.

Find out what happens when you make a habit of "getting low" to see with the eyes of Jesus.

PRAYER Thank you, Jesus, for showing me the ultimate example of how to serve. Show me how I can do it too.

DAY 336

Who are the Bible characters described below? Answer each question using Bible hero names.

1. Who was the disciple that walked on water to Jesus?
   __ __ __ __ 1

2. Who was saved from being eaten by lions? __ __ __ 2 __ 3

3. Which Bible hero wrestled wth an angel? __ __ __ __ 4

4. Which favorite son was given a coat with many colors in it?
   __ __ 5 __ __ __

5. Who did God ask to build a great ark? __ 6 __ __

6. Which prophet was swallowed by a huge fish? __ __ 7 __ __

7. Who died on the cross for our sins? __ 8 __ 9 __

8. Name the disciple who doubted Jesus was risen from the dead. 10 __ __ __ __ __

9. Name the three brave men who were put into a fiery furnace?
   __ __ __ 11 __ __ __ 12, 13 __ __ __ __ 14 __, and
   15 __ __ __ __ __ 16 __

Now fill in the letters that go with the numbers above. When you are finished, you will get some good advice.

1 Chronicles 28:20—David also said to Solomon his son,

__ '
4 8 5 10 1 6 7 16 15 7 11 14 6 7 1 15 16 8 6 9 5

__ __ __ __ __ __ __ w __ __ k. __ __ __ __ __ __
15 7 11 11 6 10 12 8   6 1   11 6 7 6 10 4 8

__ f __ __ __ __ __ __ __ __ __ __ __ __ __ __ __ '
15 1 15 11 6 1 11 2 5 14 6 9 1 15 16 8 11

f __ __ __ __ __ __ __ __ __ __. __ y __ __ __, __ __
  6 1 10 13 8 3 6 1 11 16 6 11 13   16 6 11 2 5

w __ __ __ y__ __. He will not fail you or forsake you until
  2 10 12   6 9

all the work for the service of the temple of the Lord is finished.

DAY 337

Make a list of people who genuinely support you as a Christian and who are good influencers and encouragers. Also write down what you love about each person.

_____

_____

_____

_____

_____

_____

DAY 338

For even the Son of Man did not come to be served,
but to serve, and to give his life as a ransom for many.

–MARK 10:45

A week before Christ died on the cross, he entered Jerusalem on a donkey. With all the palm-waving, cheering, hurrays, and hallelujahs, it was like one grand victory parade! People are always excited when they see someone who could claim a victory. Nobody there would have predicted that in a matter of days Jesus was going to hang on a cross. That was not the idea of victory in people's minds.

Jesus had come to Earth to die for people's sin. His resurrection was a victory over death, darkness, and sin. And it was a victory only he could claim. In his death, he served all sinners. Even though the victory came at a big price, Jesus had always come to serve.

When the Son of God doesn't look for praise but looks to serve, you know it's worth paying attention. Find out how caring for others can fill your own heart. That's worth a victory parade!

PRAYER Thank you, Lord, for sending your son to save me from sin. Because I'm so grateful, I want to serve others as well. Show me what to do.

DAY 339

But love your enemies, do good to them, and lend to them without expecting to get anything back. Then your reward will be great, and you will be children of the Most High, because he is kind to the ungrateful and wicked.

–LUKE 6:35

What's the nicest thing your best friend has done for you? Maybe she shared her lunch when you forgot yours or loaned you her spare leotard because you lost yours. In return, you got her a great birthday present. Because that's what best friends do, right? They have each other's backs.

Jesus loves it when we do nice things for our buddies. But did you know he also expects us to do the same for people we can't stand? Can you imagine everyone's confused reactions? Jesus' words were totally unexpected.

Today, they still are. Loving those who treat you poorly goes against every feeling inside you. You want to be nice to your friends and mean to your enemies. But Jesus pointed out that anyone can do that. It takes a special sort of person—a person who knows God's love and can pass it on—to love the unlovable.

Jesus doesn't stand for abuse; if someone is physically hurting or bullying you, then tell a trusted adult. But in most situations, you have a chance to shock your rivals by demonstrating kindness instead of hate—maybe even making a new friend!

PRAYER Jesus, even before we became friends, you loved me. Please help me see past my enemies' actions. Will you give me patience as I learn to love the unlovable?

DAY 340

In him [Jesus] was life, and that life was the light of all mankind. The light shines in the darkness, and the darkness has not overcome it.

–JOHN 1:4-5

Ask your mom or dad to do an experiment with you. Grab a flashlight. Head to a room you can make completely dark. Shut the curtains and doors, and put pillows or towels in front of any cracks. It has to be absolutely black. You don't want anyone to see anything at all. After a few minutes, turn on the flashlight. Ask everyone in the room what they see once the flashlight is on. Light, even the smallest one, always shows up more than the darkness. But if you shut off the flashlight or hide it under something, the darkness will be all you see.

Did you know Jesus called himself the Light of the World? He outshines sin and darkness. Neither can put out Jesus. He exposes the truth of good and evil. Wherever Jesus goes, he shines a light. The sad thing is that many people don't want to see Jesus' light. So they run away from him. Like shoving towels and pillows into cracks in a room, they shut out the light.

If you've told Jesus you want to follow him, everywhere you go you take his light—just like a flashlight in a pitch-black room.

PRAYER Jesus, light is powerful. It helps me see my clothes, what's on my plate at dinner, and where to walk. Your light is even more powerful. Let me take your light to dark places and help people discover your truth.

DAY 341

But he continued, "You are from below; I am from above. You are of this world; I am not of this world. I told you that you would die in your sins; if you do not believe that I am he, you will indeed die in your sins."

-JOHN 8:23-24

Imagine you have a bad disease and only a purple pill can save you. Now what if a friend came up to you with a handful of green, orange, and pink pills. "Pick one," your friend says. "Any one will work. I know you think only purple will work, but what about the green, orange, or pink pills? I'm sure they're just as good."

But a true friend would never do that, right? If only the purple pill will make you better, why would a friend offer you the green and orange ones?

That's the problem with other religions. It's nice to think that any religion will do, but only one takes care of our sin disease: Jesus. It's not a mean thing to say that other religions won't work; it's just the truth. And when you're dying with a disease, you definitely want the right pill to fix you up.

Be a true friend. Since Jesus is the only one who can take care of our sin problem, let's share him with others.

PRAYER Lord, help me to know how to talk to my friends about you. I want them to know that you are the only one who can fix them up and wipe away their sin.

DAY 342

Then Mary took about a pint of pure nard, an expensive perfume; she poured it on Jesus' feet and wiped his feet with her hair. And the house was filled with the fragrance of the perfume.

–JOHN 12:3

Judas was not happy. Mary had come over during dinner and poured a whole jar of fancy perfume over the feet of Jesus. Judas was steaming mad, because they could have sold the perfume, made money, and maybe put it right into his pocket.

But Jesus knew exactly what was going on with Judas. He tells Judas to leave Mary alone and he compliments Mary in front of everyone.

Jesus always notices generosity, and Mary was generous with her expensive perfume. She wanted to give her all to Jesus and it touched his heart.

What would it look like for you to give your all today? Taking time to pray? Giving some of your allowance to someone in need? Helping out your parents around the house? Whatever you choose to do, know that Jesus notices and celebrates your kindness to others.

PRAYER Lord, help me to give my all to you today. Just like Mary, I want to give my very best to you.

DAY 343

Write the words of the verse in the crossword puzzle. (Hint: Start with the longest word.)

Share with the Lord's people who are in need. Practice hospitality.

–ROMANS 12:13

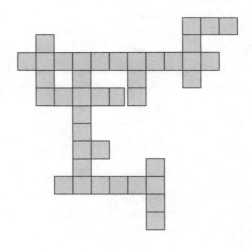

DAY 344

What does it mean to shine your light? What are your favorite ways to be a light in the darkness?

_____

_____

_____

_____

_____

_____

_____

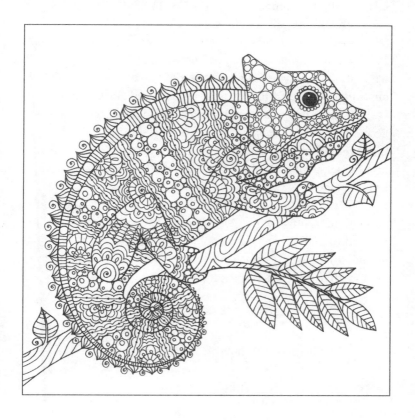

DAY 345

And I will do whatever you ask in my name, so that the Son may bring glory to the Father. You may ask me for anything in my name, and I will do it.

–JOHN 14:13-14

Jesus did the work of God on Earth. Nothing he did was out of step with his Father. In this verse, he invited his disciples (and his future followers) to do the same.

It's easy to read this verse and get caught up in the idea that Jesus will do "whatever you ask;" he will do "anything." The God who has infinite command over wind, waves, and fire, will do *anything*? You could dream up a miracle and Jesus would do it? Well, Jesus is no genie, and that's not really what the verse says. Remember, his focus on earth and in heaven is to bring glory to the Father. So when something is in accordance with his will and his character, and it brings glory to the Father, *then* Jesus assures us he'll do it.

Don't figure out what you want to do and then ask God to bless it. Instead ask what God wants to bless and go do that. Put your effort and energy into pushing open the door that Jesus has already unlocked. There is no safer, braver place to be than in God's will, calling upon the name of Jesus.

PRAYER Lord, show me how to honor you best. Give me a heart for you, so that I can do your will, walk in your ways, and be a shining light for you.

DAY 346

Then Peter said, "Silver or gold I do not have, but what I do have I give you. In the name of Jesus Christ of Nazareth, walk." Taking him by the right hand, he helped him up, and instantly the man's feet and ankles became strong.

—ACTS 3:6-7

You've probably heard the popular expression "Diamonds are a girl's best friend." Who hasn't noticed silver bracelets and gold rings on older girls you admire? A pearl necklace can make a beautiful woman look more beautiful.

But today's verses provide a picture of what is the most valuable thing you can give or receive. It has nothing to do with silver, gold, or pearls. It really has nothing to do with money. It's all about introducing someone in need to Someone who can change his or her life. That's what Peter and John did. They didn't have money or jewels to give to the beggar. But they did have the power of Jesus to share.

Most likely you know someone with special needs. That person may be blind, walk with crutches, or be confined to a wheelchair. It's also possible you know someone who is physically healthy but has an emotional or mental disability. They don't need jewelry or gifts. They need someone who treats them like Jesus would.

That could be by being a friend, helping with homework, or as easy as holding the door open. The Lord will help you know what to do. Just listen with your heart for what he will whisper.

PRAYER

Lord, forgive me for ignoring those around me who have special needs. Show me how to help them in a practical way today.

DAY 347

"Then he said: 'The God of our ancestors has chosen you to know his will and to see the Righteous One and to hear words from his mouth. You will be his witness to all people of what you have seen and heard.

—ACTS 22:14-15

Talk about a change of heart. Paul's conversion to Christ is mind-boggling—from a Christian hater to a Christian hero. Paul used to hunt down Christians to put them in jail or kill them. Then Paul became the one being hunted down by Jesus himself. Jesus told Paul that he had been chosen to know God's will and to see and hear him.

But Paul wasn't the only one Jesus chose. Jesus has chosen all of us to know and experience the very same thing. By reading the Bible, we have access to hear God speak and get to know his Son.

The other important message Jesus shares with Paul is that he will be a witness to others of how great God is in his life. What an important assignment! Telling others about his meeting with God. Paul did that very thing. He traveled for hundreds of miles and many years sharing God's story of salvation—from his own experience.

The Lord has given us the same assignment. We are his witnesses too. We simply tell what we have experienced and learned about God. Then God takes it from there.

PRAYER Lord, thanks for choosing me to know your will and to let others in on your plans for your world. It's exciting to be your ambassador.

DAY 348

Therefore, I urge you, brothers and sisters, in view of God's mercy, to offer your bodies as a living sacrifice, holy and pleasing to God—this is your true and proper worship.

−ROMANS 12:1

God has chosen people to spread his good news on earth. He wants his followers to be his witnesses, to testify about his love, power, grace, and mercy. Even though people have a tendency to muddle through, complicate life, and make relationships messy, God includes people in his plans.

James 2:26 says, "As the body without the spirit is dead, so faith without deeds is dead." God has no use for robots. He doesn't love androids. He wants living, breathing people who are capable of changing, growing, giving, contributing, and loving. No robot is blessed to do his work as the "hands and feet" of Christ because robots have not been changed by grace, hope, and mercy. But we, as his children, have been changed. We can't keep that a secret. It is our privilege to pass the good news on.

PRAYER

Thank you, God, for the privilege of life and service to you. I want to worship you with my faith and the work that comes directly from it.

DAY 349

Do not be anxious about anything, but in every situation, by prayer and petition, with thanksgiving, present your requests to God. And the peace of God, which transcends all understanding, will guard your hearts and your minds in Christ Jesus.

—PHILIPPIANS 4:6-7

There's a saying that worry is like a rocking chair. It gives you something to do but gets you nowhere. You can fret, worry, and fuss but you end up in the same place, only more tired. Prayer is totally different than worry. It does give you something to do, but, unlike worry, it gets you right where you want to be—at the feet of God.

Worry doesn't have time for the truth. Prayer is rooted in truth. Worry intensifies our anxiety. Prayer gives us a place to let worry go. Worry doesn't change anything. Prayer changes everything, because God is invited to get to work.

He not only works on your anxious circumstances, but he works on the way you *see* the circumstances. Maybe you need wisdom? He'll give it to you. Maybe you need a good dose of patience? He's got you covered. Maybe you need a whole lot of peace? He's the only one who can blanket your heart in it. Go to him in prayer and he himself will guard your heart and mind.

PRAYER God, I worry a lot. Remind me that coming to you actually changes things. Thank you for offering me peace.

DAY 350

Get along with others by remembering Romans 12:10. Unscramble the tiles. Write the correct letter in each box, and find out what it says.

Y O	T H E	N O R	A B	D E V	H O	H E R	E L V
R I	B E	N E	E A	O V E	O V E	O O	E S
N O T	N	L	D T	A N O	O N	O T E	U R S

B E							
			H O				

DAY 351

How is Jesus a hero? What characteristics of a Bible hero can you show to others?

_____

_____

_____

_____

_____

_____

— THERE IS —
NO ONE
ON EARTH LIKE
HIM: HE
IS BLAMELESS &
UPRIGHT,
A MAN WHO
FEARS
GOD &
SHUNS
EVIL.
JOB 2:3

DAY 352

*Let us not become weary in doing good, for at the
proper time we will reap a harvest if we do not give up.*

-GALATIANS 6:9

Reaping a harvest doesn't happen by accident. Before you actually get anything, there's a whole lot of dirt work—digging, turning, clearing, fertilizing. The seeds need proper care and placement. Faithful watering comes into play. And then the waiting begins. Water and wait. Water and wait. For a while, it feels like all that work is for nothing. The dirt looks the same for a long time.

And then, a sprig of green appears and we can celebrate.

In this verse, Paul compares doing good to reaping a harvest. Seeds of love grow into beauty, but they take time and effort. Do God's work and you'll reap good fruit . . . in due time. God's time. And if you don't see tangible results for awhile, don't give up. Don't get weary. Have faith that a lot is going on under the surface. After all, good fruit doesn't grow overnight.

PRAYER

Thank you, God, for the Holy Spirit who keeps me from getting weary. Show me the best way to do good with seeds of love.

DAY 353

Whatever you do, work at it with all your heart, as working for the Lord, not for men, since you know that you will receive an inheritance from the Lord as a reward. It is the Lord Christ you are serving.

–COLOSSIANS 3:23

When you find out a friend isn't feeling well, you decide to send her a package to cheer her up. As you plan it, a smile comes to your own face. As you wrap it and attach a funny card, you feel genuinely happy to be generous. You are so excited by the time you ship the package that it almost feels like *you* were the one getting a gift.

Then a week goes by. And then another week. It becomes clear that you're probably not going to hear anything back. You never sent the package to get a thank-you, but you feel your enthusiasm shrink like a pin-pricked balloon.

What started as a selfless act can feel different when you realize you had expectations of appreciation, applause, or acknowledgment. It can be distracting when people don't react the way you expect. But if you focus on working with all your heart, the reaction from people is completely beside the point. Concentrate on your effort, love, and even the fun of doing something. Then that really becomes the reward—along with knowing that the God you serve is certainly smiling.

PRAYER Lord, help me to value serving others. I know it pleases you when I focus on others. Help me be pleased with it too.

DAY 354

I urge, then, first of all, that petitions, prayers, intercession and thanksgiving be made for all people— for kings and all those in authority, that we may live peaceful and quiet lives in all godliness and holiness.

–1 TIMOTHY 2:1-2

In martial arts, the wise old karate master is called the sensei (SEN-say). That's a Japanese word that literally translates as "person born before another." Paul could definitely be considered Timothy's sensei. Timothy, a young pastor at Ephesus, frequently relied on the older, more experienced Paul for advice.

Sometimes, that advice sounded slightly crazy. For instance, Paul told Timothy to pray and give thanks for everyone, not just friends, family, and people we like. That doesn't sound so bad at first—until you consider that those are the same dudes who frequently beat the tar out of Paul and tossed him into jail!

Today we deal with many in authority. Unfortunately, a lot of them don't know Jesus. So they might pass a law we disagree with, treat us unfairly, or even bully us for our faith. When that happens, usually the last thing we want to do is pray and give thanks for them.

Yet that's what God—the ultimate sensei—asks us to do. Just like the early church, we want to live peacefully. And even though our "kings" may sometimes go against us, we are still to pray for them.

PRAYER Lord, praying and giving thanks for those who mistreat me just seems wrong. Please help me see others with your eyes, not my own, especially those in authority over me and my country.

DAY 355

. . . And I want you to stress these things, so that those who have trusted in God may be careful to devote themselves to doing what is good. These things are excellent and profitable for everyone.

–TITUS 3:8

At one time we were in complete spiritual darkness, slaves to sin. Then Christ died for us, and we became new creatures entirely. Where we were poor, we are now rich. Where we lived in darkness, we now live in light. Where we were sinful, we've been forgiven.

As children of God we have received so much, and in our abundance, we have plenty to give away. So we devote ourselves to doing what is good. Why not just stockpile our blessings and use them only for ourselves? We do what's good because Jesus lived that way, because he commanded us to, because it benefits others, and because it benefits *us*.

We are hardwired to desire meaning in life. We are designed to want a higher purpose. God gave us the desire to do good. The more we give the more we notice our rewards; the more abundantly we live, the more we *have* to give.

PRAYER

God, thank you for making me new. I love living in light and want others to know this goodness too.

DAY 356

Your love has given me great joy and encouragement, because you, brother, have refreshed the hearts of the Lord's people.

–PHILEMON 7

From the time you started playing house or pretending with Barbies, you took cues from other women in your family. You've most likely looked up to your mom, an older sister, an aunt, or maybe your grandmother. Think of those ladies who have shown you what it means to be a godly woman.

Paul had men in his life like that . . . like his good friend Philemon. Whenever Paul thought about Philemon, Paul broke into a big smile. Philemon was on his list of go-to guys. Paul didn't keep his feelings to himself. He wrote a letter to Philemon and told him how much he appreciated him.

It's important to tell people how much we appreciate them. In Paul's day, he actually wrote a letter by hand. Today we send an email or a text message. Start with "Thank you for taking time to hang out with me . . ." to show your thanks to that spiritual someone.

PRAYER Lord, I want to thank you for bringing special people into my life that help me get to know you better. Help them to feel your love today.

DAY 357

Open your Bible. Name the rulers and discover the best kind of leader.

1. This king built the first temple in Jerusalem (1 Kings 6)

2. Babylon's king took over Jerusalem (2 Kings 24:10)

3. An Egyptian king (Genesis 12:15)

4. Jesus was a descendant of this king (Romans 1:3)

5. A Roman king (Matthew 22:21)

6. The title of the ruler of Sheba who tested Solomon (1 Kings 10:1)

7. This governor reluctantly sentenced Jesus (Matthew 27:2)

1. ■ _ _ _ _ _ _

2. _ ■ _ _ _ _ _ _ _ _ _ _ _

3. _ _ _ ■ _ _ _

4. _ _ ■ _ _

5. _ ■ _ _ _ _

6. _ _ _ _ ■

7. _ _ _ _ ■ _

DAY 358

Retell one of your favorite Bible stories and share why you like it so much.

_____
_____
_____
_____
_____
_____

DAY 359

Religion that God our Father accepts as pure and faultless is this: to look after orphans and widows in their distress and to keep oneself from being polluted by the world.

−JAMES 1:27

Widows and orphans were among the loneliest people in biblical times. Society was built on family and a tight community. So when a woman lost her husband, she lost her ability to earn a living. When a child lost her parents, she lost her means of living. By losing their family, they lost their place in society and were trapped in hopelessness.

The Father wants his children to embrace the lonely, give them someone to rely on, and offer them hope. Maybe some people who are on the sidelines of society are in your neighborhood or in your classroom. I found girls who were trapped in hopeless situations in India. No matter where the need is, bring them into your circle, meet their needs with your gifts, share your abundance. As you look after them, you will love them into the arms of the Father. And they will know hope and care like they didn't have before.

PRAYER God, I know there is so much need in the world. A lot of people feel stuck and alone. I'm not sure what I can do about it, but I have a heart for them. Show me what to do.

DAY 360

Each of you should use whatever gift you have received to serve others, as faithful stewards of God's grace in its various forms.

–1 PETER 4:10

You are unique as a snowflake, a fingerprint, a new day. Your face is exclusive; your personality is matchless; your soul is exceptional. You have goals, creativity, gifts, blessings, perspectives, and experiences that are unique to you.

The Father has rained down grace on you. Now how are you going to pass that grace on?

Maybe your musical talents can bring some joy to a retirement home. Maybe your love for baking can be shared. If you enjoy being outside, you could rake the lawn of a single parent. If you like babies, you could babysit for a busy family. If you're book smart/outdoor savvy/artistic/good with computers/creative in writing/happy to be active, there is something for you to do to pass on those blessings to others. How can you bless someone?

Look around. Who needs a good dose of grace? How can you be the one who offers it?

PRAYER

Lord, thank you for all of your blessings. I need your inspiration for how I can be a blessing to others.

DAY 361

Anyone who claims to be in the light but hates a brother or sister is still in the darkness.

−1 JOHN 2:9

Stand back-to-back with a friend or sibling. Tell her to stay where she is. Then say, "I can see you." (You can't see her if you are back-to-back.) Make her try to guess how it's possible that you could see her. (It's not; you're just playing a trick.)

Did you know that people try to play a similar trick on God and on each other? "I follow God," they say. "But I hate that guy in the back row who smells like fish and chews like a cow." Hang on! How can people follow God, who is love, yet hate another person? Well, that's a problem.

Hate and love don't go together. Now, that doesn't mean that if you dislike someone you are not a Christian, but it does mean that the light of God's love has not brought you out of the darkness No one will love perfectly on earth, but when we let God into our lives and learn what his love really means, it pushes hate far from us.

So if there's someone you strongly dislike, talk to God about it. Ask him to spread the light of love in you so you can love someone who is not lovable or likeable.

PRAYER God, it's hard to pray to love someone that I really don't like. But I see how disliking someone doesn't show love. Please help me to love [fill in the name of a person you don't like].

DAY 362

Be merciful to those who doubt.

−JUDE 22

If your cousin was a record-setting Olympic gold medalist, journalists would interview him, fans would want his autograph, and fellow athletes would shake his hand. He'd appear on TV shows and in newspapers and magazines.

So what if someone said later on, "Your cousin didn't actually do that. His Olympic record sounds too good to be true.

You'd be irritated, right? "Hello, I was there!" you'd say. "I waved our flag when he won. I saw the scoreboard myself. You would never say, "Yes, since you didn't see it yourself, I can understand how it might look that way." Because why would you be understanding to a doubter?

The same reason Jude was. As an apostle, Jude saw everything firsthand. He knew people whom Jesus healed, heard the Savior's words, and watched his leader die and later come back to life. He knew Jesus was real.

Yet he still wrote, "Be merciful to those who doubt." He realized that bashing people with truth doesn't work—only grace, mercy, and love do.

PRAYER Jesus, it's so hard to understand people's hesitation about you. But I was once that way too. So until their eyes are opened, help me see them as people who need love, not judgment.

I AM ONE

DAY 364

How does God's light shine in you? How will you glimmer and shine in your life going forward?

_____

_____

_____

_____

_____

_____

DAY 365

Use the key to crack the code and find out why 1 Corinthians 16:14 gets the last word.

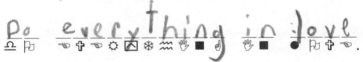

Do everything in love.

D = ♎
E = ☜
G = ♪
H = ♒
I = ✋
L = ●
N = ■
O = ♫
R = ☼
T = ❋
V = ♱
Y = ◁

Connect with Faithgirlz!

http://www.faithgirlz.com/

  www.facebook.com/Faithgirlz/

  www.instagram.com/zonderkidz_faithgirlz/

  twitter.com/zonderkidz?lang=en/

www.pinterest.com/zkidzfaithgirlz/

London Art Chase

In *London Art Chase*, the first title in the new Faithgirlz Glimmer Girls series, readers meet 10-year-old twins Mia and Maddie and their adorable little sister, Lulu. All the girls are smart, sassy, and unique in their own way, each with a special little something that adds to great family adventures.

There is pure excitement in the family as the group heads to London for the first time to watch mom, famous singer Gloria Glimmer, perform. But on a day trip to the National Gallery, Maddie witnesses what she believes to be an art theft and takes her sisters and their beloved and wacky nanny, Miss Julia, on a wild and crazy adventure as they follow the supposed thief to his lair. Will the Glimmer Girls save the day? And will Maddie find what makes her shine?

A Dolphin Wish

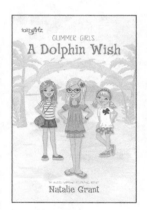

Join twins Mia and Maddie and their sidekick little sister, Lulu, as they travel the country finding adventure, mystery, and sometimes mischief along the way. Together with their famous mother, singer Gloria Glimmer, and their slightly wacky nanny Miss Julia, the sisters learn lessons about being good friends, telling the truth, and a whole lot more.

In *A Dolphin Wish*—a three-night stop in the city of San Diego seems like it might be just the break the girls need—lovely weather and great sights to see. That is until they hear animal handlers at Captain Swashbuckler's Adventure Park talking about the trouble they've been having keeping the animals in their habitats. Mia and her sisters cannot resist a challenge and they talk Miss Julia into another visit to the educational amusement park to search for clues as to what or who is helping the animals escape.

Available in stores and online!

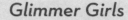
Glimmer Girls
By Award-Winning Recording Artist Natalie Grant

Miracle in Music City

In this third title in the Faithgirlz Glimmer Girls series by Natalie Grant, *Miracle in Music City*, the Glimmer Girls are at it again—looking for a mystery to solve. Gloria wants her daughters to learn they aren't too young to make a difference, so she gets them involved in her annual benefit and auction. But as things often do with the trio of smart and sassy sisters, they get themselves and their nanny Miss Julia involved in a lot more than just helping mom raise money for a worthy and wonderful cause.

Light Up New York

Join twins Mia and Maddie and their sidekick little sister, Lulu, as they travel the country finding adventure, mystery, and sometimes mischief along the way. Together with their famous mother, singer Gloria Glimmer, and their slightly wacky nanny Miss Julia, the sisters learn lessons about being good friends, telling the truth, and a whole lot more.

In this fourth book in the Faithgirlz Glimmer Girls series, the Glimmer family is headed to the Big Apple—New York City! Gloria has been asked to perform a concert in Times Square and the whole family joins her. Miss Julia immediately starts planning a sightseeing trip for the sisters that will be better than all the rest, but plans never turn out exactly as they imagine when the Glimmer girls are involved. So what happens when sibling rivalry, random acts of kindness, and a little mystery all meet up at some of the most famous sights in New York City?

Available in stores and online!